THE POWER OF STANDING IN FAITH

The Ultimate Test

By: Paola A. Hasbun

Copyright © 2013 by Paola A. Hasbun

The Power of Standing in Faith
The Ultimate Test

by Paola A. Hasbun
Cover Design by Chloe St. Ettienne

Printed in the United States of America

ISBN 9781628390209

All rights reserved solely by the author. The author guarantees all contents are original and do not infringe upon the legal rights of any other person or work. No part of this book may be reproduced in any form without the permission of the author. The views expressed in this book are not necessarily those of the publisher.

Unless otherwise indicated, Bible quotations are taken from the New International Version (NIV). Copyright © 1999 by Vida.

www.xulonpress.com

Acknowledgements

First of all, most importantly, I want to give praise, glory, and thanks to my eternal, heavenly, Father God and His Son Jesus Christ for the opportunity of writing this book and being able to share it with the world. I also want to give thanks to my parents and brothers, for having unfailing love for me. For all my family members, church friends and mentors, and everyone who prayed for me during my treatment, may God bless you always. Thanks to all my distant family members, who came to visit me during my treatment, Tia Ivannia and Tia Malena and family I love you so much. A special thanks to Pastor Aldoin and Dee Boudoin, Mike and Kathleen Williams, and Ross and Celeste Trahan for truly being there for my family and I in the toughest time, praying for us, serving us, and coming to visit and help us out during our transition. As well as all the members of Grace Community Church who prayed for my treatment to go well. I also want to thank Mrs. Emily Zavala for helping us in constant prayer, support, and encouragement during and after our time of need. For Dr. Jerry Kramer and my English Professor, Gina Palmer, who graciously edited the book.

Also thanks to Chloe Saint Ettienne for taking the time to design the cover. And of course, to all the caring and diligent staff at M.D. Anderson Cancer Center, thank you.

Table of Contents

Chapter 1	Knowing 9
Chapter 2	The Beginning. 22
Chapter 3	M.D. Anderson Cancer Center 29
Chapter 4	The Power in Standing in Faith 37
Chapter 5	Beginning Treatment. 45
Chapter 6	Adjusting to Change 62
Chapter 7	Salvation 67
Chapter 8	Miraculous 85
Chapter 9	Challenge over Challenge. 93
Chapter 10	A New Beginning 98

Preface

What does a beginning mean to you? According to the Merriam-Webster Dictionary to begin means "to do the first part of an action; beginning: to come into being." According to the Bible, in the first Book of Genesis, the beginning of the world and humanization is described in great detail as God created life as we know it. Ironically, the beginning for my life was when I was told it was the end as I was diagnosed with a malignant brain tumor. Everyone has their own beliefs, their own memories, their own experiences, and their own stories. This is mine.

"For I know the plans I have for you," declares the LORD, "plans to prosper you and not to harm you, plans to give you hope and a future." Jeremiah 29:11. God loves you so much and wants the best for you. The purpose of this book is not to judge, lecture, or guilt trip anyone. The purpose is to simply show you the miracles the Lord Jesus Christ has done in my life. With a God so great full of abundant love and mercy how could I be so selfish in not telling you about His magnificence? God has a divine purpose for you and wants you to know His plan for your life and to live for Him. I found God in the trial of having cancer and being treated for it. He showed me His love, grace, and mercy during the toughest time in my life.

God is three in one, the Father, God, the Son, Jesus Christ, and the Holy Spirit. When Jesus left, He sent the Holy Spirit to comfort, counsel, and help us, as John 14:16-18 states, "And I will ask the Father, and He will give you another Counselor to be with you forever — the Spirit of truth. The world cannot accept him, because it neither sees him nor knows him. But you know him, for he lives with you and will be in you. I will not leave you as orphans; I will come to you." The Holy Spirit also reveals truth to us and teaches us, as John 14:26 states, "But the Counselor, the Holy Spirit, whom the Father will send in my name, will teach you all things and will remind you of everything I have said to you."

Will all your problems and troubles be gone once you accept Jesus as your savior and ask for the Holy Spirit? Of course not. The Christian life is challenging, and sometimes we fall, but that is when the Holy Spirit comes to comfort you and tell you, "You can do it, get up!" You can talk to your friends about God. You can say no to alcohol and drugs. You can say no to premarital sex. You can love your enemies, all with the help of the Holy Spirit. Like the disciple Paul states in Romans 7:15-17, "[15]I do not understand what I do. For what I want to do I do not do, but what I hate I do. [16]And if I do what I do not want to do, I agree that the law is good. [17]As it is, it is no longer I myself who do it, but it is sin living in me." What Paul is trying to express is the constant battle between the flesh and the spirit; what he (the flesh) wants to do is not what he does and what he does by the spirit, is not what he wants to do.

Chapter 1

Knowing

There are opportunities in everyone's life when he or she must choose either to ignore the truth and continue to walk in sin or wake up from that illusion of a righteous life and change. But the truth is that no one can change by his or her own will. You can only change with God's intervention and transformation. I have seen there are three types of people. The most common type of person is the one who lives in sin, knows that it is wrong, but does not attempt to change. The other type of person recognizes his or her faults early and tries to change. The smaller group of people, are those who are significantly affected and afflicted by a certain event, which God uses to change them from the inside out, to live for Him. I fall under the third category of people.

I could never be able to explain the complete serenity and peace that I experienced when I gave my entire life to Jesus, when I was saved. Only God can fill you with complete faith, trust, peace, and love for Him. We are truly saved by His grace, as Ephesians 2:8 states, "For it is by grace you have been saved, through faith—and this not from yourselves, it is the gift of God." God is giving you a gift, He is not going to knock on our door and remind us that we have to go to church and read the Bible. We have to pursue Him. My intention is not to lecture or to preach but to tell you about the miracles God has done in my life. It is truly impossible for the human mind to comprehend God's planning and His choices.

My personal experience of amazing grace began in February of 2008, when I was diagnosed with brain cancer at the age of sixteen. I was a normal high school student at Benjamin Franklin High School in New Orleans. My family and I had been living there since I was in second grade when we moved from West Haven, Connecticut. I have two younger brothers, Roberto, who is currently sixteen and Felipe, who is currently twelve. My mom is Costa Rican, and my dad who was born in El Salvador, is half Palestinian and half American. I was born in Galveston, Texas, moved to West Haven, Connecticut, for five years, and then lived in New Orleans for nine.

When Hurricane Katrina hit in 2005, we moved to Lafayette, Louisiana. There we started attending a church called Grace Community Church. When we moved back to New Orleans, for my freshman year of high school, we continued to go to Lafayette for church, driving two and a half every Saturday night or Sunday morning. My family traveled to Lafayette because the place where we lived was relaxing and peaceful to my parents and siblings, and being there prevented me from going to parties and doing other things of which my parents did not approve. However, the main reason was to attend a church that truly drew us closer to God.

In Lafayette, we lived in a mobile home on a farm that we bought. The property is four acres and included a small lake. My brothers never complained about going, and the place itself was secluded and peaceful, except to me. I hated being away from my friends over the weekend. I felt that I deserved to do what I wanted due to how hard I worked during the week and the recurring notion that I would be young only once and needed to have as much fun as possible. Every weekend we went to Lafayette and every weekend I got infuriated. I could not stop yelling and complaining, and sometimes I would cry. I was completely blinded by the devil. The idea about being young only once and having to experience anything you want is a lie of the enemy. Once this idea became implanted in my mind, I began to let my joy, mood, and attitude depend on the activities I did and with whom they were done. An even worse result of this mind set is participating in events you would not have engaged in before.

A common example is doing drugs. How many teenagers in America begin to do drugs when they are young? According to www.teendrugabuse.us/teendrugstatistics.html teen drug use as of 2003 was 30.3% in 8th graders, 44.9% in 10th graders, and 52.8% in 12th graders. At the high school I attended for two years in New Orleans, several students used marijuana and a few students used more potent drugs and even died from overdoses. Using drugs like any other sin is a weapon of the devil to bring bondage over your life in order to sink you closer to your eternal damnation. Every decision brings a consequence. As Galatians 6:7 reads, "Do not be deceived: God cannot be mocked. A man reaps what he sows."

My story began after our family moved to Lafayette, Louisiana because of Hurricane Katrina. Slowly, but surely, my arrogance grew as I began to surround myself with the wrong crowd. When we moved to Lafayette, we bought a nice home with a big backyard as well as a mobile home on a farm in Broussard, Louisiana. The mobile home was about twenty minutes from our church. So, when we came to Lafayette on Saturday night, from New Orleans, I would either spend the night at my friends' house or stay overnight in the mobile home with my family. Then, on Sunday mornings, we would go to church. I used to think that church was fake and that it was impossible for people always to be smiling and to be happy. Even though the sermons were great, I was blinded by the enemy, and kept ignoring what God kept trying to say to me. After church, my parents and I would talk to some close church members, including Mike and Kathleen Williams, Ross Trahan and his wife Celeste, and Pastor Aldon and Dee Boudoin. It took about a year for us to be close, but the time we took driving every weekend and going to church was more than worth it. After about a year of getting to know each other at church, we start making plans out of church.

One Sunday night, on February 10, 2008, after coming from Lafayette, I start having a painful headache. I still had an Algebra test and a Chemistry quiz to study for, but I could not study because of the intense pain. I could not go to school the next day because of the pain in my head. For a while, I kept asking myself if it was a type of stress headache, but it was a new type of pain, much more severe. I woke up the next morning with an even greater headache. This was not like a normal migraine headache, the front and sides of my head were in intolerable pain. I literally felt like my head was going to explode. There was an unimaginable pressure in my brain that I could not begin to explain. When I got out of bed, sat in a chair, moved too fast, or bent down in the slightest way, my headache would worsen. My eyes were light sensitive; using the computer increased my pain. On Tuesday, February 12, 2008, the headache got worse and while I was reading something on the computer screen, I began having trouble reading the words. I was vaguely experiencing double vision and vertigo.

On Thursday, my headache became unbearable. My dad scheduled an urgent appointment with my pediatrician. Before I left, my friend called me to tell me that one of my teachers told the students that if you had an extra day to study for a test, he would make the test harder, by not allowing you to have bonus points, it would not be multiple choice, and you would have to show all your work in the same period of time. With the intense headache that I had, I got out of bed, to send my math teacher an email. The moment I stood up from my bed I felt like I was going to vomit. Every step running to the bathroom made my head hurt even more. The pain escalated as I vomited. Even though I was sure the school and my teachers knew, I sat in front of the computer, and sent my teacher an e-mail explaining my absence and telling him that the second I could take the test I would. He did not answer, so I re-sent it, but he never replied. Right after sending the e-mail to my teacher for the second time, I sent one to another teacher just to inform her of the situation. She also did not reply.

The enemy always uses little things like that to take away our peace and to take our focus off God. As Song of Solomon 2:15 reads, "Catch for us the foxes, the little foxes that ruin the vineyards, our vineyards that are in bloom". We cannot allow little and insignificant problems steal our peace and make us anxious. As Philippians 4:6-7 reads, "Do not be anxious about anything, but in everything, by prayer and petition, with thanksgiving, present your request unto the Lord. And the peace of God that transcends all understanding will guard your heart and mind." We cannot let the devil control our lives. As Christians we have agreed to follow Christ and with it comes many tribulations, as Ephesians 6:12 reads, "For our struggle is not against flesh and blood, but against the rulers, against the authorities, against the powers of this dark world and against the spiritual forces of evil in the heavenly realms." We need to put on God's armor every day and fight to follow Him. As Ephesians 6:14-17 reads, that we need to put on "the belt of truth", "the breastplate of righteousness", "the helmet of salvation", "the sword of the spirit", "the shield of faith," and with our feet we should spread the word. And as Ephesians 6:17 reads, "Take the helmet of salvation and the sword of the Spirit, which is the word of God."

My father was a doctor at the Tulane Medical Center. He had scheduled the appointment with my pediatrician, Dr. Alicia Diaz-Thomas. She is sweet, humble, and friendly, and her love for her patients radiated through her. Dr. Diaz began asking me about my symptoms. Was I experiencing any dizziness?, Have I had this pain before?, Was I experiencing any blurred vision? After all these questions, Dr. Diaz just stared at her notes for about thirty seconds;

she slowly raised her head, looked at me, and asked, "Do you think you have a brain tumor?" I was caught off guard and shocked by her question. I simply answered, "Oh no, of course not." According to Dr. Diaz's assessment, there was nothing wrong. But she said that to be on the safe side, she would schedule a CT scan for the next day.

That same day, Valentine's Day, my parents had invited some family friends from our church in Lafayette for dinner in New Orleans. They ended up staying overnight. When I woke the next morning, Friday, February 15, I could barely lift myself up from my bed. My head felt heavy, full of inexplicable pain. I was lying awake in my bed for about two hours before our family friends came to say goodbye. Before they left, they all gathered around my bed, with my parents, and prayed for me. One particular prayer caught my attention; "Heavenly father, we pray for whatever is causing this headache to be revealed to us through the CT scan later on today." My father did not tell me then, but he told me about a few weeks later, that the second those words were prayed over me God revealed to him that something was wrong.

I had expected for my headache to be better and for me to go to the school's sweet sixteen party the next day. I had already bought the dress, the shoes, and had my hairdo planned. The truth is that we can't determine for certain that something is going to happen; it's always if God permits it to happen. Today, I could not be happier that God gave me a second chance by giving me a brain tumor. I never thought in any way that it was a punishment and later realized that it gave me a second chance to live for Him. Before going through treatment, I was a completely different person than I am now. I was rude and arrogant and I lied constantly. I also drank alcohol with friends almost every weekend, I smoked cigarettes occasionally at parties, I cursed, I disrespected my parents all the time, I was inconsiderate, I rode in friends' cars speeding up to 80 mph in a 40 mph zone, and I went to unedifying parties almost every weekend. Sure, at the time all of that was fun, because our body is made from the flesh, constantly driving us to put our desires into action, but we need to constantly fight and pray at all times in order to have the Holy Spirit within us, as 1Thessolonians 5:17 reads, "[16]Be joyful always; [17]pray continually; [18]give thanks in all circumstances, for this is God's will for you in Christ Jesus."

    Every minute that passed increased the pressure I felt in my head. My mom told my father to see if it was possible to reschedule the CT scan earlier. He was able to change it from 5 p.m. to 11 a.m. I had to move very slowly and make sure I did not walk too fast in order to refrain from intensifying my headache. My mom helped me walk, holding on to my arm and waist. As my parents and I entered the radiologists' clinic, I noticed that my mom was crying, but she did not tell me why. All she said was that these tests made her nervous.

Months later, she told me that while entering the clinic, she had a vision of me in a white hospital gown with no hair and a nurse rolling my wheelchair. As we waited in the lobby for the CT scan, my mom would not let go of my hand.

When someone called my name, a very friendly nurse came out and asked me to please change into a robe. I was very calm as I lay down on the CT bed. The exam was very easy and it only took ten minutes. After the test, I got out and sat with my parents. In about five minutes, a radiologist came and called to my dad to speak to him. My mom and I waited in the lobby. Ten minutes passed. As we continued to wait, twenty more minutes passed, and finally an additional half an hour while we were waiting for my dad to come out. My mom and I kept telling each other that there must be something wrong because of the amount of time they were talking together. He finally came out with a mournful look on his face. His eyes were sad, filled with hopelessness, and he sounded as if he were holding his tears in as he said, "Es un tumor", or "It's a tumor." Immediately, my mom responded with a mixture of anger and tears, asking him if he was sure. The moment I heard my dad say those words right there in the middle of the waiting area, I began crying and screaming, saying, "I don't want to die, I don't want to die." My parents kept telling me that I was not going to die while attempting to console me with their love.

My mom gently escorted me outside the clinic to take a walk. I remember holding very tightly to my mom while I was hysterically crying and hyperventilating. I kept asking her, "Why me? I'm a good person?" "WHY ME?" For a while my mom just kept telling me that everything was going to be all right. She said that when God started something, He finished it. She also told me that God had a purpose for everything. I was crying and sobbing while walking through downtown New Orleans and thinking to myself, I love my family too much, I do not want to die, and I cannot imagine being without them. The thought of my family without me was unbearable. I kept picturing my parents' pain when I was dead. I thought of everything I had planned for my life and how meaningless it was now. I kept thinking of how unimportant things of this world were. However, what caused the most pain was thinking of how I would be without them.

Before we got back to the clinic, we stopped at a small bar and restaurant. We sat down and were silent until the waiter came. My mother ordered a crawfish bisque, and I ordered blackberry ice cream and lemonade. I ate a few spoonfuls and drank a few sips of my lemonade. When my mom tried to swallow her soup, her throat did not allow it. My mom told me later that she was incapable of swallowing as if there was a block in her throat. She did not tell anyone at the time, but she felt as if God was telling her that she needed to fast that week. My dad found us and came in to the restaurant and sat with us for about ten minutes. Then, he took us back to the clinic.

When we returned to the clinic, I start to relax. The radiologist told my dad that I needed to get an M.R.I, or a Magnetic Reasonance Imaging exam, in order to determine the exact location of the tumor. Since I was little, I had always had a phobia of needles. This time they had to put in an I.V. to do the brain M.R.I. with contrast (the contrast allows the radiated part of your body to be shown clearer). My mom came in with me and held my hand until the M.R.I bed moved into the covered "tunnel." When, you are in the M.R.I, a mirror reflects what is right outside the tunnel you are lying on. As I went in, I began to cry softly as I saw my mom and thought of the life changing morning I had had.

My brothers, Roberto, who was fifteen at the time, and, Felipe who was eleven, reacted in very different ways. Roberto, to whom I was really close, had friends over when I got back home from the M.R.I. He simply came up to me privately and said, "Hey, do you have a brain tumor?" I just looked at him and said, "Yeah". Felipe on the other hand, was a little more emotional about the situation.

He came up to me very sweetly and gave me a hug. He had a look of worry and love that was purely innocent and caring.

Chapter 2

THE BEGINNING

The diagnosis was completely life changing. Every time that I took a step, my headache got worse; step-by-step, I started to stop taking things for granted. The same day I was diagnosed, my dad arranged for me to see the Chairman of Neurosurgery from Tulane. After analyzing all the tests and details, Dr. Melgar told us that the tumor was 2.3 cm wide and that it was located in the middle of the brain in the third ventricle and that the tumor was causing obstruction of the spinal fluid causing hydrocephalus. According to the American Heritage® dictionary Hydrocephalus is usually a congenital condition in which an abnormal accumulation of fluid in the cerebral ventricles causes enlargement of the skull and compression of the brain, destroying much of the neural tissue. This was the cause of my severe headaches. Thank God we found out that I had this at an early stage before my skull expanded or before I had metastasis, or a spread, of the brain tumor.

The Beginning

I finally got to the room, which was honestly a complete miracle. The fact that I was diagnosed, consulted with the head of neurosurgery at Tulane, and admitted to the hospital on the same day was all a miracle. God opened all the doors. he knew how urgent this first surgery was. I was admitted at the intensive care unit immediately. I did not have my own room. There were curtains that separated the other patients from me. There was this small plastic moveable toilet on my left, the monitors were on the right, and the curtain right in front of me was where the doctors, nurses, and family or friends would come in.

That night, I met two really nice and interesting nurses. My main nurse was Keera and my other nurse was called Maja. Keera came in with Maja a few times, a couple hours after my parents left. I stayed up all night talking to them. We talked about my trips to Costa Rica, life, and the future. Once in a while Maja would leave, but Keera stayed all night in my room comforting me. I really needed that attention and loving comfort since my parents were not allowed to stay with me in the I.C.U. Of course she left to go to the bathroom and to check on the other patients once in a while, but from 6 p.m. that night until 1 a.m. when I went to sleep, they were in my room, listening to what I had to say. I honestly felt like it was a sleepover. They were angels that God sent me. By the time she left, I had her number, and we had plans to go to The Melting Pot Restaurant when I was ALL done with treatment.

The first surgery, the endoscopic third ventriculostomy, was quick. God allowed Dr. Melgar to successfully make another pathway for my cerebrospinal fluid that was being blocked by the tumor. To explain in a little more detail, my tumor was in the middle of my brain, which was blocking the pathway of cerebrospinal fluid in my head. According to the American Medical Dictionary, Cerebrospinal fluid is a liquid that is continuously produced and absorbed, which flows in the ventricles, or cavities in the brain and around the surface of the brain and spinal cord; it provides nutrients to the brain. My head was literally being expanded as the C.S.F., or cerebral spinal fluid was being accumulated. This type of pressure in my brain was referred to as hydrocephalus. Hydro means water and cephalus means head in Latin. The pressure that I felt was a permanent feeling of an explosion or like a bomb going off in my head constantly. The endoscopic third ventriculostomy was the surgery that was necessary to perform in order to create a new pathway for the C.S.F., to stop the hydrocephalus.

The endoscopic third ventriculostomy was an alternative to having a shunt put in my brain. A shunt is a plastic catheter, or tube, that carries cerebrospinal fluid from a ventricle in the brain to another area of the body made of plastic. There is a high chance of infection with having a shunt in the brain. Thank God that He used Dr. Melgar's hands to successfully perform an Endoscopic Third Ventriculostomy surgery. He told my dad that he would treat me as if I were his own daughter. Another surgeon would most likely have just given me a shunt, because only 2% of the neurosurgeons in the United States know how to perform an Endoscopic Third Ventriculostomy with out placing a permanent shunt in the patients brain. It was a complete miracle and blessing to fall into the hands of a surgeon who could!

The next day, Dr. Melgar told us that he scheduled the surgery on March 17, 2008, the following day. Before the surgery, I had to take a lot of exams, but before that, some friends came to visit me. They brought me a few magazines, different colored Twizzlers, M&Ms, blush and nail polish. We talked about the dance the school was having for Sweet Sixteen. They told me what they were going to wear, and who they were going with. As they were talking about their dresses and how much they were going to miss me, I realized that there are so many more important things to worry about, and for me it was my health. When they left, they told me they were not going to tell anyone and that they were going to pray for me.

After they left I had to take a few tests. I took a urine test, they took my vitals, drew my blood, and gave me an I.V. Drawing blood was ridiculously painful, so was the I.V. The nurse at the pre-op surgery clinic missed the vein not once but twice, so they had to poke me three times with that long sharp needle to draw the blood. I felt like I was going to pass out, because I was terribly scared of needles. After they poked me the first time, I was crying and tense, just imagine after the third poke! The first surgery was a breeze. The anesthesia did not hurt through my I.V. I did not feel any pain after I woke up until five hours later. I was taking Toradal for pain and Tylenol with codeine every six hours. After surgery that night, I stayed as an in-patient. My parents brought me dinner and we watched two movies. Before my parents left, we read the Bible and prayed. The next day we had a visit from a church friend from Lafayette. He prayed over me and inspired me to think positively about this diagnosis. I decided to look at this time in my life as a step that I had to pass like my mom had suggested earlier. What I did not know was that this "step" was truly going to change my entire life in every possible way, from my morals and beliefs, appearance, and attitude to where I lived permanently.

As I prayed more and read the Bible more, God began to reveal to me several things by allowing the Holy Spirit to remove the blinds covering my eyes and let me see what was really going on around me. It reminded me of how unimportant earthly things are when it comes to being true and close to God. Why should we risk having our only TRUE friend, our only TRUE love, and our only TRUE

Father , or popular in the world where the devil controls society? At this moment, I knew God was starting to change me.

My mom made my room at the hospital so beautiful while also bringing me new warm pajamas, slippers, and the Bible at my reach so I could read it whenever I wanted to. It is incredible how much my parents did to bring me comfort in that time of my life. My mom was always there unless she urgently needed to go attend to my brothers and all my family came in the evening to eat with me, read the Bible, and pray. After about a week of recovery from the first surgery, Dr. Melgar planned to do the next one, the brain biopsy. In order to know exactly what kind of tumor I had they had to remove a part of it and examine it. Thank God both the third ventriculostomy and the brain biopsy went well with no symptoms or problems. By the time I was done with the first two surgeries, I looked completely different. Before I was diagnosed, I had long auburn wavy hair that reached to my lower back. Before the first surgery, my mom brushed all my hair back and made a braid. My hair had been shortened to my shoulders and was donated to the Locks of Love Organization. It was no longer wavy but curly.

For the first surgery, they shaved my head from above my nose all the way to the end of my scalp. For the second surgery, they went through the same hole they had drilled in my skull for the third ventriculostomy. The second time, my wound got infected. I was taking Levaquin and Zyvox, which are very powerful antibiotics. Dr. Melgar told us a number of tumors that I could have, but he mentioned that my tumor looked like a germinoma, because it was shaped as if it were a butterfly. A germinoma brain tumor is a benign tumor and could be treated just with radiation and chemotherapy. There was also a possibility for my tumor to be a very malignant one, which would obviously have greater effects on my health and treatment.

One of the days while I was inpatient, I walked around the floor with my parents. Part of my head was shaved, I had a large gauze on my wound with iodine, which looked like blood, and antibiotic cream was spreading from under the gauze. While I was walking, this little three-year-old boy came in the opposite direction with his mom. He could not stop staring at me, I cannot blame him. I just felt like laughing, so I rolled my eyes and lifted up my hands and said, "Oooooohhh", as if I were a Zombie. That little boy grabbed his mom's leg so tight and looked so scared that he had to stop looking at me and closed his eyes. God knows I did not mean to scare the little kid, I just wanted to laugh in that critical time. While I was recovering in the hospital, the biopsy sample of my brain was being sent to M.D. Anderson Cancer Center in Houston, Texas.

Chapter 3

M.D. ANDERSON CANCER CENTER

When I got back home from the hospital, I start to sleep in my parent's room in a separate bed in order for my parents to keep an eye on me. As I was recovering from the first two surgeries, our family prayed that the tumor would be the easiest one to be cured from, the Germinoma. When my mom told a Christian friend of hers that we were praying for it to be a Germinoma, she told my mom, "Why do you limit God's power? He doesn't need it to be a benign tumor to heal her, pray for there not to be any tumor; don't pray for a type of tumor." She was so right! We were limiting our faith by praying for a benign tumor instead of a malignant tumor. We desperately waited for a little over a week for the result of the brain biopsy to come back from Houston. As we were waiting, I was recovering and researching chemotherapy.

When I heard that I needed chemotherapy, I made sure I knew what I was going to go through. Since I was a needle phobic at the time, I looked up "chemo syringes" on Google images almost every day. I expected chemotherapy to be ten times worse than it actually was. I expected them to put a frightening I.V. in my neck in order to get to a major artery for the chemo. Then, I thought that the chemo would burn my veins. I was extremely frantic about the idea of needles in my skin. I also thought that I was going to vomit everyday and finish weighing close to eighty pounds.

One of the hardest things for me at that time was imagining myself being bald! I had long, auburn, wavy hair that reached a little higher than my belly button. I was almost obsessive over my hair. About a year before my diagnosis, I was at a salon with my mom getting a haircut. One of the hairdressers said, "What if I got all your hair in a braid and chopped it all off?" I responded, "Oh yeah right, that's never going to happen."

Something similar to this happened when my dad was dropping me off at school. I had been really rude and arrogant with my mom one morning. That morning, when my dad was driving me to the bus stop, he parked and told me that I could not keep up this attitude, this arrogance. He said, "You have to change." While my heart was breaking in pieces, knowing how much I was hurting my parents, without being able to stop, I said, "Pa, I was born arrogant and I'm always going to be arrogant; that's how I am."

God heard both of my responses about the hair and the arrogance and decided that he was going to do something. I acknowledge that my tumor was not a punishment, but a second chance to live the right way, following what Jesus had ordered us all to do. Even if I could, I would have not taken my tumor away. In only one year, God completely changed me. He changed my values and morals in every way, my personality, and my complete way of thinking for good. But most importantly, He spiritually saved me, all thanks to His mercy and grace.

About a week after my biopsy, I headed to my parents room to see where they were. I found my mom crying on her bed with my dad by her side consoling her. I immediately asked her what was wrong. She told me that we did not get good news from M.D. Anderson and that if the tumor was a malignant one, the whole process of healing could be more risky and dangerous. M.D. Anderson had sent news that the tumor was not a Germinoma, but a malignant Pineoblastoma brain tumor.

That same night that we found out about my dangerous diagnosis, our family left for M.D. Anderson in Houston. We found out at about seven p.m. and immediately packed our bags, my dad made an appointment with a pediatric oncologist at M.D. Anderson Cancer Center , and we left our house in New Orleans at 10 p.m.

We did not know where we were going to stay, what school my brothers were going to go to, and my dad left his job without knowing if he was going to be able to have one in Houston. All we knew was that it was a life threatening emergency for me to be treated as soon as possible. And our neurosurgeon in New Orleans, Dr. Melgar, said that if I were his daughter, he would bring me to Houston to be treated for cancer. So we took his advice. We left for Houston, six hours from our home, completely unaware of what was going to happen or how long we were going to stay. We were only capable of such a leap of faith by holding on to the promise that God will take care of His children. We had complete faith that He was not going to let anything bad happen to us.

After driving for hours, we stopped in Beaumont, Texas about two in the morning. We found a hotel and slept a few hours because we had to wake up early to drive to Houston for my appointment with my future pediatric oncologist, Dr. Johannes Wolff. The next morning, we drove the rest of the way without any problems thank God.

I remember driving up the parking lot of the M.D. Anderson Cancer Center. I was staring out the window at the enormous facility and thinking of everything that I had to go through to get to my goal of being healed. God gave me faith and peace and I was not scared in any way, but curious about my new change of lifestyle. As we parked, my mom made sure I did not fall by gently holding on to me.

The second we entered the main entrance of the hospital, I was completely amazed. It was enormous, but welcoming at the same time. There was a hospital volunteer playing beautiful relaxing songs on the piano and there was a serene fountain in the middle about eight feet tall. The tranquil aura filled the room. It did not trigger a frightening emotion when I walked in, like other hospitals had made me feel before. God blessed me with such a wonderful hospital to be treated in.

After we had lunch in the lobby, my pediatric oncologists and his nurse practitioner came all the way down to meet my family and guided us to the pediatric floor. Even though they had a busy schedule, they both personally came down to meet, welcome, and guide us. That act of kindness that they showed was only a preview of their consideration, love, and determination for their patients.

The first time I went to the pediatric floor was even more surprising than entering the building. There was a bald girl walking in her pajamas attached to a chemo pole by a small transparent tube- like cord. The tube went from the bag of fluids, through the machine and then under her shirt. As the machine began to beep, a nurse came to change one of her bags of fluid.

The floor has a family room, where the patient's families eat, a teen room, where patients go to play games, use the computer, watch TV, eat snacks, etc. There is also an art room for the younger patients. In it are coloring books, construction paper, crayons, board games, a Wii, etc. There is also a large room on the floor called the Pedi Dome. The ceiling is painted with clouds and there are four large windows towards the back of the room that light up the whole space. There are about four small toy bicycles for toddlers, a playhouse with several toys, and a basketball hoop and air hockey machine for older kids.

There is also a school that consists of two rooms on the floor that helps children continue their schoolwork while being in treatment. They have a special program for children in elementary and middle school. The school has several programs that teach the patients that attend there. They have a writers group in which two teachers come to educate the children at school about writing. Several volunteers come to help and give time to the school's needs and the students there. They have a writing, a science, and an art program that visit once a week. Volunteers also come on Fridays for cooking class. The school also host several parties in which they decorate the Pedi Dome. For example, the end of the year party, a Christmas party, a Halloween party, a Thanksgiving party, etc. They also have random parties such as the New York party, China party, etc. For the China party the whole Pedi-dome was covered with grey imitation brick paper to represent the Great Wall of China. They had a show of Dragon dancers, Chinese food, games; a raffle was going on, etc. MD Anderson also receives many visits from famous people. When I was in treatment, the Latin Grammys came, the Astros, Miss Texas, a renowned group of cyclists that bike to Alaska every year, and the Daughters of Liberty organization came as well to show the patients antiquated quilts of their ancestors. Several volunteers and donations play a huge part in having all the blessings and comfort that the patients receive during treatment.

Child life is also located on the pediatric floor. Child life is basically in charge of the patient's comfort. They bring movies and or games to the patients' room; they're in charge of the teen room, art room for the kids, the Pedi Dome parties, decorations on the floor, etc. They really have a huge part in the positive environment that the patient is treated in.

There is also a staff for the school. I can personally say that they all have showed love, care and consideration at the most acme point. They have never been rude or arrogant. On the contrary, they put themselves in the patient's shoes, befriend them, and never pass any sort of judgment. If the patient needs help in something, they will stop whatever they are doing to help. I have honestly never had such a blessing with any other teachers in my life.

Chapter 4

THE POWER IN STANDING IN FAITH

The day that I was admitted to the hospital, my doctor contacted a neurosurgeon to tell him about my case. He said he would bring me up at their board meeting to see who can and who would operate me. Throughout the elongated week of waiting, we got different responses from my doctors on whether or not I was going to have the surgery.

After a week of constantly praying for the board meeting to approve of my surgery, my doctor informed us of the decision not to operate on me, because it was too risky. I did not know at the time, but my dad had read in the past month that without surgery with this type of tumor there was a fifty percent mortality rate. That same day, the doctors planned for the beginning of treatment for me with Proton Radiation and Chemotherapy.

Our family could not and would not accept this death sentence, so we continued to pray and asked relatives and friends around the world to do the same. We prayed for God to touch one of the neurosurgeon's hearts to give him compassion and decide to go against the final decision and offer surgery for me. We had the complete faith that I was not going to die from this and that God was going to touch one of the doctor's hearts.

My dad kept sending e-mails asking for a chance for the surgery. After about three days, a neurosurgeon, Dr. Jeffrey Weinberg, contacted my dad to tell him that he would do my surgery. He told us from the beginning that it was going to be risky and that we would have to sit down and talk about all the adverse symptoms I could have. He told us he would come down to the pediatric floor the next day.

Monday passed without his visit, then Tuesday, Wednesday, Thursday, and Friday. I was in-patient in the hospital. My parents were trying to balance taking care of my brothers, being with me, and making meals as we waited for the neurosurgeon to stop by. Finally, on Saturday, God reveled to my parents what we needed to do. My mother told my father to do something about it and he did.

While I was inpatient, my father sat at a computer outside of my room and sent the Dean of M.D. Anderson Cancer Center a respectful and wise e-mail telling him about our treatment situation. The next morning, at seven a.m., Dr. Weinberg showed up at our room very humble and apologetically. He told us that he had a hard week and that he was sorry for making us wait unannounced for so long. We forgave him and understood his situation. We need to forgive and forget, especially if they apologize. Is that not what God does with us every day?

Later on the same day, we had a meeting with him. He explained to us the procedure that he was going to perform in my head and how risky it was. We needed to sign several consent forms to make sure we would not sue him if anything went wrong. Each consent form was protecting him and his staff from any legal penalties for any adverse symptoms that I could have obtained from the surgery.

I was luridly calm and peaceful when the doctor read the entire list of symptoms that I could have attained from the surgery. Some expected symptoms were: kidney failure, sterility, necessity of a hearing aid for the rest of my life, etc. The more severe expected symptoms were: blindness, deafness, kidney failure, liver dysfunction, becoming mute, mentally retarded, paralyzed in a wheel chair the rest of my life, having a stroke and there was a shocking and terrifying high percent chance of death.

After hearing and signing all the consent forms and hearing all the possible adverse symptoms, God gave me a complete peace and never allowed me to fear. I never thought of how they were going to remove the tumor. He used my parent's calmness and lack of sadness to encourage me that I was going to survive and recover fast after this surgery. Going into the surgery, I honestly felt complete tranquility and serenity. There was no fear to be found, thank God.

My parents called ALL our family and friends to pray for me. They also sent mass e-mails to everyone on their contact list. They asked their families, friends, coworkers, and church members to pray for my surgery to be successful and for a fast recovery. Church friends from Lafayette, Louisiana came to Houston to be there for my surgery and help us in anything that we needed. My Aunt Ivannia, on my mom's side, also came from Switzerland to help with taking care of my brothers during my surgery. My other Aunt Malena, on my dad's side, also came to help us out in anything we might need. They were both very helpful, loving, and caring always.

The day before my surgery, we had a pre-op appointment to explain to us what we needed to do and at what time we had to arrive at the clinic. They told us that I had to be in NPO coming into the surgery, which meant that I could not eat or drink anything after midnight the day before the surgery. They also said that I could not use any lotion, perfume, or deodorant the day of the surgery, as well as brush my teeth, just in case any paste was swallowed.

On March 19, 2008, we woke up at four thirty a.m., read the Bible, prayed, and got ready to go to the hospital for the pre-op anesthesia at six a.m. Thank God we arrived on time and were right on schedule. The nurses asked me to change into a robe and later came in to give me an I.V. in my right arm. After I changed, they asked me to get on a movable bed. The nurse rolled me to the waiting area for patients that just went through pre-op anesthesia, waiting to go into surgery. A nurse came up to me and asked me if I wanted to color something while I was waiting to go in. She gave me a coloring book to choose drawings from. I chose to color a bunny in a meadow using different colored crayons.

After coloring, before the surgery, the nurse asked my parents to please wait out in the waiting area because they were bringing me in shortly. My parents both gave me sweet and tender goodbyes as they left the room. Earlier and at the current time, I did not think about how they were going to remove the tumor, it did not occur to me that in order to remove the tumor that was in the middle of my brain that they actually had to open my skull. I guess I assumed they were going to suck it out of my ear or something. I thank God for that innocent ignorance He gave me that was key to the peace He gave me.

My faith in God and unawareness was a great comfort before and during the time in the waiting room. Nurses kept comforting me asking me if I was scared. I simply said no and stated Romans 8:31, "If God is with me who can be against me?" I did not even think of the high percentage of dying, I knew that God was not going to allow this to be the end of me. But there was one superfluous thought floating around in my mind about one of the symptoms mentioned on the list, the hearing aid. I kept picturing myself at my wedding in the future when the groom would say "I do". I kept seeing myself bending towards him in this beautiful white dress saying, "I what? I what?" I was focused on such an insignificant matter, which God used to distract me completely of the dangerous and unexpected success of a twelve hour open skull surgery.

Before the surgery, my parents and Christian family friends prayed over my neurosurgeon's hands for God to use them to resect the cancerous tumor from the middle of my brain completely without any unwanted adverse symptoms. After the surgeon left, they all kept praying and fasting in the surgery waiting area.

In the surgery room, I was blessed with having two nurses that helped me get onto the surgery table. My two nurses were gentle, loving, and caring. I asked them to please make sure I was not uncovered in any way during my surgery. They were understanding and helpful in every way possible. I remember the pain of the anesthesia before falling into a deep sleep. It was an excruciating burning pain going into my vein. I kept telling my nurse that it burned repeatedly until they put an anesthesia breathing mask over my head and fell asleep. My nurse kept telling me that it would soon be over, and it soon was.

After twelve long and nerve racking hours, my surgery was over. They operated from eight a.m. to eight p.m. When I woke up, I thought that I was going into surgery and that it never happened. A male nurse kindly told me that it was over. He was rolling me to see my parents in the I.C.U., next door. The second I saw my mom, I began to move my neck from left to right saying, "Mami my neck, my neck, it hurts." I can only imagine my mom's happiness and joy when she saw that I was alive and that I was talking and moving. She immediately raised her hands and praised the Lord Jesus. It was a phenomenal miracle!

When they moved me to the I.C.U., my pediatric oncologist came and ordered them to give me a morphine pump. Every fifteen minutes, the green button would go off for me to press it in order to receive more morphine. After about an hour, I could barely see anything, I had complete blurry vision. My aunt came to say goodbye, because she had a plane to catch back home. I remember seeing a dark blurry figure with her gentle voice coming from it. After an hour of being on the morphine pump, my mom told the doctors to get me off it, because I had had enough and that I felt better. She was worried of me getting addicted to it. The morphine made me feel lethargic, completely useless, and absolutely out of self control. It was an awful sensation.

After a twelve-hour craniotomy surgery, it was expected to stay at least two weeks in the I.C.U. and two months on the pediatric floor. However, we continued to pray from the beginning for a fast and complete recovery and thanks to God I was in the ICU for only three days and on the floor for less than two week. I was out of the hospital in less than a month after an expected over a month recovery in the hospital. Both my Jewish neurosurgeon and my atheist oncologist said that they should start to make praying a routine before the surgeries, because they had never seen such a miraculous surgery, fast healing, and recovery in the past, thank you JESUS! And the best part of the whole thing was that God used the neurosurgeon's hands to remove ninety-seven percent of the tumor, even though it was attached to main veins and arteries, was two point three centimeters in length, and an over fifty percent chance of dying, praise GOD!!! God does not have any limits for anyone, especially for those who have faith. The only limit God has is the one you put over Him through your lack of faith.

Chapter 5

BEGINNING TREATMENT

After the Craniotomy, the neurosurgeon put me on a steroid called Dexamethasone, which helped reduce the inflammation of the brain. Before I was diagnosed, I considered my friends and my health as priorities. I was highly competitive in sports. I woke up every morning at 5 am to run three miles on our treadmill, did crunches, pushups and arm exercises. I would come home, after walking eleven blocks from the bus stop, get on the treadmill again, run three more miles, go walking to our gym, swim laps, and if I had time, I would get on the elliptical. Shortly, before I got diagnosed, I began taking kickboxing class on Mondays and Salsa classes on Thursdays. I was on the volleyball team freshman year and loved to run. Just to give an example, in seventh grade, I ran in a seventh and eighth grade division of a hundred and fifty-two girls. I placed second from only being twenty seconds behind the winner.

The point is, when I came to M.D. Anderson for treatment, I was a healthy one hundred thirty- five pounds.

It was the brain tumor that kept me from being skin and bones while I was exercising, so much was because of the brain tumor. For the past year and a half before being diagnosed, I was craving sweets that I had never craved before. When my friends brought cakes, brownies, and cupcakes for one of our birthdays, I would rarely reject them and then feel guilty when I got home and exercised more.

I later found out that the tumor had been growing in my head for a year to a year and a half and that it was growing on sugar. So, I was craving sweets day and night, which I had not before. I still remember some midnight snacks I had with my brother, before I was diagnosed with the brain tumor. I would dip carrots in peanut butter, put Nutella and or peanut butter on bananas and gulp them down with a glass of milk.

If I had not been so determined about my exercising, I would probably have weighed 176 pounds without steroids. While I was visiting relatives in Costa Rica, the summer before the diagnosis, my second cousin told my mom in private, "Paola should watch how much she is eating, because the way she is eating will bring her to obesity." She was right. I would take breaks throughout the day just to eat. I would play volleyball on the beach, eat, swim, eat, walk, eat, etc.

Then, as part of my pre-chemo treatment, I had to take steroids. I found myself eating three times as much because of the constant, unsatisfied hunger. One time, my dad came home while I was on the steroids and asked me if I was hungry. I told him that I was not exactly hungry at the moment because I had just had a snack. He then asked me what I had eaten and I simply said, "Oh, just two bagels." My dad erupted in laughter at how hungry the steroids were making me.

I went from a healthy hundred and thirty-five pounds to an unhealthy hundred and seventy-six pounds in less than three weeks. I was huge. I had a double chin, puffy cheeks, and to top it all off, I got stretch marks everywhere. God touched my pride in having long beautiful hair and being physically fit. I was large and bald.

The first surgery I went through at M.D. Anderson was my port-a-cath surgery. In order to receive chemotherapy treatment, I had to have a port-a-cath for the chemo to go through my veins and arteries without burning them. A port-a-cath is a medical device used to administrate chemotherapy easier. It is approximately three inches wide and three inches long. It consisted of a circular piece of plastic with a gel center. It also has a small tube attached to the middle of the port. For receiving the chemotherapy, a catheter, or syringe, is injected in your upper chest area, the catheter injects under the skin, and through the gel part of the port, which goes into the small tube into the veins and arteries.

The surgery was very quick. I went in, changed out of my clothes, put on patient scrubs, my family and I prayed again, and then the anesthesiologist put me to sleep. I was in and out of the surgery room in less than an hour and went down to the floor for treatment that same day. The only thing extremely painful about the surgery was the soreness I had in my chest after they stitched the port-a-cath to my right breast muscle.

I could not move my arms in any way because it increased the pain in my chest. Just washing my hands or brushing my teeth was extremely painful. This soreness lasted for about five to seven days. My mom even had to help me take my shirt off when I wanted a shower. God truly humbled me by my not being able to take care of myself and needing others to help me.

A port-a-cath is much easier on a patient than having to be stuck with a needle every time there was a need to draw blood. When I was in chemotherapy, my port became accessed because I needed labs, or blood drawn, every day for the doctors and nurses to see how my blood counts were doing. The port was really convenient when I had it; however, the first time it was accessed was one of the most painful experiences of my treatment.

When I went to the Pediatric Oncology clinic, after having the port-a-cath surgery, I was told that the first time I had my port accessed had to be done by the I.V. team. No one warned me that this team usually worked only with adults and were less compassionate. One of the most painful moments I had during treatment was definitely my first port access in the clinic by the I.V. team.

I remember lying down in a room in the clinic, when an older Asian nurse came in with a two inch thick catheter in her hands. I tried my best not to think of the pain awaiting me. I introduced myself, and so did she. I asked her to please be gentle, but she acted as if I had said please be rough, brutal, and inhumane. I do not think I screamed and cried at the top of my lungs during any other incident as loud as I did when I was accessed for the first time by that lady.

I remember lying down and telling myself it was not going to hurt. But as soon as she began feeling for my port by pushing it into my chest, I lost hope and knew it was going to be bad. One of my favorite nurses, Rachael, was right next to me holding my hand, and my mother was on my right holding the other. In order for them to inject the catheter in the right place, I had to stay very still and move my shoulders back to push the catheter upward.

I remember the first rapid and violent stab she injected over my port-a-cath. I began screaming in an outside voice. She was injecting and pulling it out so fast that she kept missing the middle of the port-a-cath, I would not be surprised to know that she got it in the right place and accidently pulled it out again. She did not even check if it was placed in the right spot. She simply continued to stick and unstick me until my screaming was loud enough for the whole floor to hear me yelling. When the time she finally got tired of injecting me, she pulled the catheter out violently, right after I told her to please be gentle.

By the time the I.V. nurse was done drawing the labs, Rachael looked like she was about to punch the I.V. nurse and my mom was infuriated, as it was if she wanted to grab her and beat her to the floor. The I.V. nurse had roughly and briskly injected me NINE times until she decided that she found the port. I do not know if she thought I was made of plastic or if I did not have pain receptors. That woman was definitely the worst nurse I had in all my experience during my treatment. I remained bruised and in pain from the surgery as well as the first port-a-cath access for about a week and a half.

About a week or two before I started chemotherapy, I started treatment with Proton Radiation to terminate any malignant cells that were left from after the surgery. Proton radiation therapy is a form of external-beam radiation treatment. In my case, large machines generated beams that penetrated my body from the outside. There are only twenty-five Proton Radiation Centers in the world, and M.D. Anderson is one of the first places to have it. It was an extraordinary blessing to be able to have access to M.D. Anderson's Proton Radiation Center.

Beginning Treatment

My first appointment, at the Proton Radiation center was to make a mask. The mask is necessary for the patient to use while the radiation is taking place in order to keep me still. The mask is strapped to the bed used in radiation. After the nurse called me in, I had to change into a gown. Then the staff personnel, told me to lie down in a room where metal was not allowed. At the beginning, rays of light began to draw upon my body. Then the nurse came and drew, with permanent marker, on my face and then drew a line going down to my stomach. The next day they sculpted my mask, and finally, on the third day, I began treatment.

The treatment plan time was Monday-Fridays for six weeks. The appointments initially lasted an hour, but later on, during the last week, they went down to forty-five minutes each, the booster appointments. However, the waiting time usually beat the actual appointment time. The waiting time was always a hassle unless you called early, which we learned to do when we were finishing the treatment. Many patients arrived late, so appointments became delayed for the rest of the patients.

Even though the waiting time was usually long, the waiting area was really peaceful. There were always several interesting magazines. Coffee and hot chocolate were available, and when someone finished treatment, the patient's family usually brought food. Cake was the favorite. There is also an area with a computer and kids reading books and playing games and a water fountain in the middle of the large waiting area.

All my appointments were all in the evening around five thirty to seven P.M. I usually came to the appointments on an empty stomach because one of the treatment's side effects is nausea. The other side effects of treatment are: fatigue, itchiness, burnt skin, vertigo, dark lines on skin, and skin rashes. Thank God, I never experienced any vomiting or painful skin symptoms, which any cancer patient will tell you is truly a miracle.

I began chemotherapy while I was taking proton radiation treatment. Due to the fatigue caused by the radiationthey brought on all I wanted to do is sleep. My first chemotherapeutic treatment started in March of 2008 and I stayed on the pediatric floor for a week. I had light nausea from a level of three out of ten, ten being vomiting, throughout the week. During my first chemotherapy treatment, all I did was lie down and watch movies and sleep. I would wake up late, order breakfast from the hospital's room service, read the Bible, pray, talk to the group of doctors about my symptoms and go back to sleep with an I.V. Benadryl. During chemo, I could not sleep without getting I.V. Benadryl. It not only helped prevent nausea, but also made me feel as if fairy dust for sleeping were being sprinkled over me. I never missed the chance to ask for it when I could; thank God it's not a narcotic, in which I could have grown addictive to it.

Between the end of the first chemotherapy and the second chemotherapy treatment, I went to the hospital only for check-ups and treatments. They drew blood from me a minimum of three times a week to check my white cell count, hemoglobin, protein intake, etc. When I was in-patient, they checked it every morning at four a.m. at the same time when they weighed me. The chemo plan was for me to be in-patient for one week every month for eight months.

The second chemotherapy treatment was the worst one because of the drastic increase in the number of chemo drugs. However, I was not surprised. I was previously warned of the intense nausea that was going to come. Even though my brain tumor is extremely rare, our family met another patient who was finishing their treatment who had the same diagnosis as mine at M.D. Anderson. It was a blessing to get to meet him and his family.

We met in the most random and strange way. About two weeks prior to when we met, we knew we existed; the doctors told us there was another patient with our same diagnosis. The doctors couldn't legally tell us their names but they vaguely described us to each other. They knew that I was a seventeen year old girl and I knew that the other patient was a seventeen year old Turkish boy.

One day, my mom and I were waiting in the Pediatric Oncology Clinic for an appointment. I needed to have blood drawn to check my cell counts. While we were waiting in the clinic, this woman leaned forward from her seat towards my mom's ear and randomly says, without ever speaking to her before, "My son has a brain tumor too." It was completely random, awkward, and unexpected for her to say that. My mom gently leaned over towards her and said in a confused and stunned manner, "I'm sorry, what?" After she repeated herself, my mom introduced herself first and then, she told us their story. She came with her husband and only son to get the best treatment for him. He was diagnosed with a rare and malignant Pineoblastoma as well. When I went to my appointment, my mother and Angel stayed talking and getting to know each other.

I received the most amounts of chemotherapeutic drugs in the second cycle. In a span of a week, I received the most powerful chemo drugs. Some of these potent drugs are Vincristine, which effects your nervous system and gives you needle like pain sensations throughout your body, Cisplatin, which is known for giving dire nausea and damaging your hearing, Cyclophosphamide, which causes your kidneys to hurt, Methotrexate, which usually causes decreased kidney and liver function, as well as Ifosfomide, Etoposide, and Isotretinoin. The last four drugs don't have a specific side effect that

I noticed; they all caused a mixture of different side effects, such as: nausea, fatigue, loss of appetite, kidney and bladder pain, diarrhea, fever, hair loss, joint pains, numbness and tingling sensations, rash, ringing nose in ears, hearing loss, vertigo, low white and red cell counts, low platelets, etc.

Vincristine only runs through your line for twenty minutes while you are in-patient due to its level of potency. The main symptom a patient receives is peripheral neuropathy, or numbness, tingling, and dreadful needle pains all over your body. This drug is probably the most potent one I received. It can only be given in extremely low doses for only a short period of time. When I was inpatient for my week of chemo, I only received Vincristine one day for about twenty minutes. It's currently been eight months since my last treatment of Vincristine and I still get needle pains a few times a week.

Another powerful chemotherapy drug is Cisplatin. In my opinion, this medication does the most damage. On top of all the expected symptoms, nausea, vomiting, fatigue, loss of appetite, etc. it is known for causing ringing in the patient's ear and hearing loss. The medical staff also told me that it is usually the chemo drug that gives the patient the most nausea. When I was inpatient for treatment, I received Cisplatin for three days and it took two hours to enter my body safely. By the end of taking Cisplatin for eight cycles of chemotherapy, I ended up with minor permanent hearing loss in my right ear, which wasn't noticeable by others or myself. But after praying for a complete healing, after six months, the Otolaryngologist technician, told me that she did not know what happened but the hearing loss was completely gone and that my hearing was back to normal, thank God!

Methotrexate was expected to cause kidney and liver problems. In my case, in one of the later chemotherapy treatments I got terrible pains in my lower right abdomen. It lasted for only three days, thank God. I drank plenty of water to wash out my kidney and took some medications my doctor gave me. Ifosfamide had similar side effects as Methotrexate, it was expected to decreased kidney function and give bladder irritation constantly.

The list of side effects can go on for pages; I experienced almost all of these symptoms. One symptom that doctors couldn't believe that I never had during my chemo cycles inpatient was vomiting, which is a complete miracle. I was nauseated all the time I was awake during chemotherapy, but God helped me not to think about it and distracted me from actually vomiting. Thank God for all the medications he has allowed to be invented to prevent nausea during chemotherapy such as: Emend, Protonix, Odansetron, or Zofran (all oral medications) and Benadryl (IV), Phenergan, Ativan, Aloxi, etc. The Zofran was something I had to take twice a day every day for nausea, Protonix was taken once daily for acid reflux, and the Emend was taken before chemo started, for nausea; everything else was only given when needed.

I also had a few shots to help me during treatments. At the beginning of my first chemotherapy, a gynecologist came up to my room. She informed us of the risks of having your period during chemotherapy. Chemotherapy already drops your blood counts, having your period at the same time would be too dangerous. So, she said that I needed to have the Lupron shot three times, once every three months in order to stop my menstrual cycle.

The first time I got the Lupron shot was during one of my chemotherapy cycles while I was inpatient. My parents and I had been waiting all day for the shot to come. It was finally ten pm, which was past the latest visiting hours. After we read the Bible and prayed, I said goodbye and goodnight and the shot never came. I had to constantly go to the bathroom because of the fluids I was getting overnight for hydration. At one in the morning I carefully got out of bed, sore from the port-a-cath surgery and went to the bathroom. About five minutes after I got back into bed, my nurse knocked on the door and came in with the Lupron, a huge intramuscular shot. She told me that it finally had arrived from the pharmacy and that it was doctors' orders to give it to me as soon as it came in.

The second I saw that syringe I began to cry. First of all, I had always been scared of shots, second of all, my parents were not there to give me support, third of all, I was in dire pain from the port-a-cath surgery and could barely move, fourth of all, the syringe was extremely long and had several milliliters of medicine to inject, and fifth of all, it was an intramuscular shot! Since, it was intramuscular, my nurse asked me if I wanted it in my leg, my stomach, or my butt. I immediately asked her which one hurt less, but she did not answer me. Since I was in such pain from the port-a-cath surgery, it was almost impossible for me to lie down on my stomach. That same day, my mom told me that it was better to get it in the butt. Before I attempted to roll over on my side, the nurse suggested putting it in my leg. So then I asked her for some numbing Emla cream. After having the Emla cream for an hour and a half on my leg, which is the required time, I was still not ready emotionally for the shot. She suggested numbing the skin even more with a bag of ice. I left the ice on for a good twenty minutes and I was still very nervous.

When she took the bag of ice away, started cleaning the skin with alcohol and took out the twenty gage needle, I began to hyperventilate and cry even more while asking her, "Could you please count to three, could you please flush it in slowly, could you please be gentle?" The second I felt that thick and heavy vaccine enter my body, I began to scream and cry. Not only did I still feel that huge needle go into my skin, but because the medication was so thick and cold, it burned like fire, stung like a thousand wasp bites, and hurt like a knife stabbing me over and over again.

After the shot, she told me that I was really brave and brought me a mini horse stuffed animal, as if I was two years old. I was limping for three days due to the soreness caused by the shot and was still sore from the port-a-cath surgery. I was later so disappointed when my mother told me that the nurse should have made me turn on my side to get the shot because it would have dramatically hurt less. My mom, being an I.C.U. nurse, knew that the nurse had to know that it was less painful to have the shot in my butt or stomach. Just to think that I could have prevented all that pain by praying with faith to God, made me upset as well.

Even though my mom told me that the butt or stomach was the best place to get the next Lupron, I got it in the arm. I was defiantly not crying as much as the first time and I had my parents with me. The third and final time I got the Lupron shot was on my bottom in November of 2008, when I was finishing chemotherapy. This time, thank God, it was half the pain from the one before.

There were several other medications that I took daily other than ones for nausea. Since the chemotherapy weakened me in every way possible, I had to take a magnesium protein complex twice a day, every day, Bactrim, to prevent infections, three times a week twice daily, and K-Phos tablets daily, twice a day, to give me potassium and phosphate, which the chemo was killing. Later in my treatment, I start taking Lyrica for neuropathy pains and headaches that I got frequently.

I also took other medications to help with my treatment. My Pastor's s wife in Lafayette, Louisiana, suggested taking natural medications on top of the ones prescribed by the doctors. We talked to our doctor and got all the list of new medications approved by him. I began to taking both the hospital's medication and the natural ones.

We ordered 12 different natural medicines, 8 of which I took. I began taking 2 liquid ones, 1 powdered, and 5 capsules. The 3 medicines that I dropped were PH Greenzone, Black Walnut extract, and Chinese Mineral-CHI Tonic. The PH Greenzone claims to provide high-alkaline nutrition, support normal-range blood sugar levels, helps cleanse and detoxify the body, and promotes energy, endurance, and stamina. This medicine is powdered and needs to be shaken in water or juice. The Black Walnut Extract which claims to support the immune system in its battle against infection, soothes irritated tissues, enhances the look of the skin, and help maintain the intestinal system. It had a bitter and dry flavor to it. It is a liquid that could be mixed with water. Another natural medicine I never even tried was the Chinese Mineral –CHI Tonic that claims to boost the potassium level in your body.

The medicines that I took daily were Silver Shield, Bifidophilus Flora Force, Gaba Plus, Colostrum with Immune Factors, and All Cell Detox. The All Cell Detox claims to cleanse the colon, liver, kidneys, aid digestion, and promote the absorption of nutrients. It is thought that Colostrum stimulate cytokines, key immunological factors, protect the overall health of the gastrointestinal tract, promote normal bowel function, maintain the intestinal lining, and boost muscle growth due to increased secretion of a growth factor. The Gaba Plus claims to support brain and nerve metabolism, normalize nervous system function, and promote a greater sense of relaxation and peace. The Bifidophilus Flora Force claims to improve immune system function, promote intestinal health, help promote respiratory health, and help systemize B vitamins. And finally, Silver Shield that claims to help immune system with a non-toxic efficiency. All of the medications I took were capsules except the Silver Shield. It came in small glass bottles filled with clear liquid that does not taste like anything. I took a teaspoon with every meal, three times a day every day.

Chapter 6

ADJUSTING TO CHANGE

My doctors could not believe that I still had my eyebrows and eyelashes during the third chemotherapy cycle. On the other hand, the hair on my head was abundantly falling out every day. One day, while I was home in Houston, I woke up and saw a huge chunk of hair on my pillow. My mom said that just looking at it was traumatizing and that she thought it would be better if she just snipped all my hair off. The chunks of hair falling from the sides of my head were certainly troubling. However, the huge impaired lengths damaged from shaving parts off for surgery were even more upsetting to look at. I had shoulder length hair with a straight line shaved in the front, from where I got my third ventriculostomy and my biopsy, and in the back where I had my craniotomy. On top of that, clumps of hair were on my pillow every morning, and in the shower, and on the sofas. While taking showers, I had to make sure to pick up all the hair that fell. Just running my fingers through my hair made huge amounts of it fall off. By the beginning of the fourth chemo, however, all my hair on my head had fallen out. I remember how weird it felt to take showers with a bald head after having had such long hair.

I was not comfortable with going out in public bald, so we bought a wig. However, the wig not only demanded care but was very uncomfortable. I remember walking in the first wig store and seeing how expensive and ugly the wigs were. In the second store we went to I found the wig I was going to buy. It was a black straight-haired kind a little longer than shoulder length.

Since the wigs were too tight, itchy, and uncomfortable, I settled on wearing chemo hats. The first one came from a donation box in the Pediatric Oncologist Clinic. My mom then knitted eight chemo hats for me during all the time she was with me in the hospital. She even went to knitting classes to learn how to make the hats and to make me a coat. Every time we would go to the clinic or when she came with me to the hospital when I was inpatient, she knitted.

About two weeks after the craniotomy, my neurosurgeon scheduled a date to remove the staples and stitches from the back of my head. When I was told that those staples were not degradable, I began to worry if removing them would hurt. I kept pestering my parents, doctors and nurses, and other patients who had already gone through this experience. I remember starting to count down ten days early.

On the same day I went wig shopping, the neurosurgeon's assistant removed the staples from my head. I remember walking into my neurosurgeon's clinic for the procedure. I prayed for a miracle beginning the week before that I would not feel any pain during the removal. I also prayed for a gentle and kind nurse to do the job.

When I found out that my doctor's young nurse was going to remove them, I became really nervous, because I had been praying for the older, experienced nurse to pull them out. My parents calmed and encouraged me by telling me that a younger nurse would likely be more careful and kind, as she had been earlier. Then Ms. Amanda came carrying a packet of utensils. The instant I saw all those tools, my heart began to beat twice as fast. Removing the staples and stitches required me to lie on my side. When I lay down, I started praying. I kept repeating in a low voice, "Jesus, you are my healer, my redeemer, my beautiful savior God, please send an angel to hold my hand. God, I ask in Jesus name, send an angel to console me, God, please!" I said that prayer over and over again in different tones of whisper.

I was astonished at what God allowed to happen because of His love and the faith He gave me. I felt a peace surrounding me that He was taking care of everything, and then I knew that I was holding the hand of an angel I could not see. I kept lifting my hand, holding on to His presence and His wonderful angel who came to comfort me. I felt no pain even when one of the stitches stuck to my skin and was dug out, pulled out, and snipped. The only experience that made me cringe during the process was the noise and sensation of the staples being clipped in half and pulled out, but, thank God, I did not feel any pain. Ms. Amanda was gentle and did a great job, thank God!

When I left the clinic, I was overwhelmed with gratefulness to God, who had freed me from the extreme pain I thought I would experience. Mark 9:23 reads, "Jesus said unto him, 'If thou canst believe, all things are possible to him that believeth'." Mathew 21:22 also talks about the result of believing and trusting God "If you believe, you will receive whatever you ask for in prayer." Even though I was anxiously counting down almost two weeks before the day of my procedure, God gave me faith, and I believed in my heart that He would not let me feel any pain.

Psalm 119:71 truly applied to my life: "It was good for me to be afflicted so that I might learn your decrees." If I had not gone through treatment for cancer, I would have continued to live in sin until I died and would not fulfill God's purpose for my life. If I could go back in time and change something, I would have tried to draw myself closer to God and to grow a relationship with Him, but I would not change my diagnosis. I could not be more thankful that God gave me a second chance to live for Him. He warned me before the diagnosis, to change, but I did not listen. Why do we have to face afflictions to make us change? Why can't we just listen the first time and save ourselves so much trouble, sadness, and time? Are we scared of change or of ridicule by other people? Romans 12:2 states, "[2]Do not conform any longer to the pattern of this world, but be transformed by the renewing of your mind. Then you will be able to test and approve what God's will is—His good, pleasing and perfect will."

Chapter 7

SALVATION

During my fifth chemotherapy, my life experienced a turning point that only God's love could have brought about. It was about 7:45 p.m. on April 8, 2008 when I got saved. That special day, while I was inpatient receiving chemotherapy at M.D. Anderson Cancer Hospital, truly was the gist of my life. My family and I were reading a scripture in Matthew during our Bible study time at night when the Spirit of God permeated in me. I began to think of God's mercy, grace, and love and of Jesus' overwhelming ultimate sacrifice. I felt a love, peace, and joy that no material thing or person could EVER give me. It filled me as water fills a glass. His touch is powerful, calming, and absolutely ethereal. As my face continued to drop tears of joy, love, and adoration, I called my pastor, who was having dinner with other church members, and told them what God had done for me.

God had not only healed me physically, but He had also changed my soul by giving me the gift of salvation. I could write a billion words a day and never be able to explain God's presence. He is so loving, tender, merciful, caring, faithful, and beautiful that our minds cannot possibly comprehend. Nevertheless, trying to explain His greatness, which I must do, draws His presence to me, and my face becomes drenched in tears of serenity, joy, and thankfulness. It's as if your soul is stripped to the very core and then filled with abundant and infinite love and peace.

The second the presence of God touches you, your life will never be the same. All you need to do is humbly open up to Him, seek Him, follow Him and give Him FULL authority over your entire life, all for His glory. We need to learn to have and exercise the fruits of the spirit. The Bible states in Galatians 6:22-26, "But the fruit of the Spirit is love, joy, peace, patience, kindness, goodness, faithfulness, [23]gentleness and self-control. Against such things there is no law. [24]Those who belong to Christ Jesus have crucified the sinful nature with its passions and desires. [25]Since we live by the Spirit, let us keep in step with the Spirit. [26]Let us not become conceited, provoking and envying each other."

The Epistle to the Romans, in chapter 10: 9-10, explains how we can be saved: "[9]That if you confess with your mouth, "Jesus is Lord," and believe in your heart that God raised him from the dead, you will be saved. ¹⁰For it is with your heart that you believe and are justified, and it is with your mouth that you confess and are saved." We have to seek Him in every situation, during every time of the day, in making every decision. We need to hold on to Him for strength and courage to stand up against dangerous secular beliefs in society and stand firm in God's word through acts of spiritual love. Early in the morning, before we eat breakfast or get ready for the upcoming day, we should make it our first priority to spend time with our loving Father He is the most important One of all and is more than worthy of our time!

Of course, living the Christian life seriously and vigilantly is not easy. Who wants to wake up a half an hour or even an hour before they are supposed to in order to read God's word and to speak to Him? That is why we need to pray constantly for God to help us dominate the flesh and to fill us with His amazing love to get up and glorify God in every way, no matter the time or effort we need to put into it. The best times I have had with God are early in the morning with my door closed and the rest of my family asleep. The Bible reads in John 15:19, "¹⁹If you belonged to the world, it would love you as its own. As it is, you do not belong to the world, but I have chosen you out of the world. That is why the world hates you." God clearly states that being a true Christian is hard. Mathew 6:33 declares, "But seek first his kingdom and his righteousness, and all these things will be given to you as well." The Bible also states in Mathew 5:6-7, "And when you pray, do not be like the hypocrites, for they love to pray standing in the synagogues and on the street corners to be seen by men. I tell you the truth; they have received their reward in full. [6]But when you pray go into your room, close the door and pray to your Father, who is unseen. Then your Father, who sees what is done in secret, will reward you. [7]And when you pray, do not keep on babbling like pagans, for they think they will be heard because of their many words." Would we rather sleep an hour more each night and not experience God's saving, healing, love, mercy and presence? Let's not allow the devil to fool us into thinking that going to church every Sunday is enough. Proverbs 6:9-11 reads, "How long will you lie there, you sluggard? When will you get up from your sleep? [10]A little sleep, a little slumber, a little folding of the hands to rest — [11]and poverty will come on you like a thief and scarcity like an armed man." We need to be devoted to God, give beyond 100% in everything we do and know that if we are being obedient to God, He is going to help us.

When God saved me, He gave me a passion to spread my testimony, or miracle story, with everyone and never lose an opportunity for God to use me to open someone's heart towards Him. All of my old shame and embarrassment about speaking of God have been removed, thanks to Jesus.

Before I was saved, I was an utterly, unbelievably different person in and out. I used to be arrogant, selfish, prideful, disobedient, disrespectful, and inconsiderate. I used vulgar language and cursed, complained over everything possible, I was never optimistic and was always stressed and worried about everything and anything since I can remember. I was always a "what if" person, having no faith that God was going to come through for me.

Your parents, your friends, your pastor or your siblings can tell you that you are doing something wrong and that you should change, but ONLY God can change you. Instead of fighting with a people about reforming, we should lift our desires to the Lord and pray for them. My parents were sick and tired of my arrogance, rudeness, and fastidious, demanding behavior. I used to yell at my mom constantly with such a haughty tone that she would be in tears by the end of our arguments. I will always regret treating such a loving, caring, and sweet mother that God gave me so awfully. All I know is that I have already repented of all my sins and God has forgiven me. God has forgiven me and my old self is gone, so why should I live in the past? I am a new creation in Christ; the old me is dead, and the new me is alive and seeking the magnificent presence of Jesus Christ. Ephesians 2:1-10 reads, "As for you, you were dead in your transgressions and sins, [2] in which you used to live when you followed the ways of this world and of the ruler of the kingdom of the air, the spirit who is now at work in those who are disobedient. ³ All of us also lived among them at one time, gratifying the cravings of our flesh and following its desires and thoughts. Like the rest, we were by nature deserving of wrath. ⁴ But because of his great love for us, God, who is rich in mercy, ⁵ made us alive with Christ even when we were dead in transgressions—it is by grace you have been saved. ⁶ And God raised us up with Christ and seated us with Him in the heavenly realms in Christ Jesus, ⁷ in order that in the coming ages he might show the incomparable riches of his grace, expressed in his kindness to us in Christ Jesus. ⁸ For it is by grace you have been saved, through faith—and this is not from yourselves, it is the gift of God— ⁹ not by works, so that no one can boast. ¹⁰ For we are God's handiwork, created in Christ Jesus to do good works, which God prepared in advance for us to do."

Everything about your life changes when you are saved. You have an overwhelming desire in your heart for a personal intimate relationship with Jesus Christ. God gives a joy in removing all the destructive relationships and bad habits from your life. Instead of sadness at "missing out" with friends who were spiritually bringing me down, He gave me the immense joy of being able to live for Him. I realized that while it is important and wonderful to have friends, we need to pray for wisdom and revelation in choosing our circle of support.

We need to remove all those people in our life who make us sin, because just as God uses people to glorify Him, the enemy also uses people to bring us down and doubt God. We need to be grounded and to pray, "Holy father, precious Jesus, thank you for everything you bless me with, because I know that everything I own is yours. God protect and accompany me in this every new day and guide me through your path. Make me spiritually strong and brave not to fall into temptation. Give me wisdom and an abundance of your Holy Spirit. You are awesome, Jesus, and I love you more than any material thing or person." You just need to close your eyes with devotion and talk to God through your heart, and He will give you the desires of your heart according to His will. The Bible states in Psalm 37:4, "[4]Take delight in the LORD, and he will give you the desires of your heart." You could also pray the Jesus prayer in Mathew 6, "Our Father in heaven, hallowed be your name, [10] your kingdom come, your will be done, on earth as it is in heaven. [11] Give us today our daily bread. [12] And forgive us our debts, as we also have forgiven our debtors. [13] And lead us not into temptation, but deliver us from the evil one."

It is possible to understand this message in two different ways. The first is God is with me, so I do not have to do anything. Or you can interpret it the right way by doing your best in everything you do in the name of Jesus and know that He will help you do everything according to His will. James 2:14-17 states, "What good is it, my brothers, if a man claims to have faith but has no deeds? Can such faith save him? [15]Suppose a brother or sister is without clothes and daily food. [16]If one of you says to him, "Go, I wish you well; keep warm and well fed," but does nothing about his physical needs, what good is it? [17]In the same way, faith by itself, if it is not accompanied by action, is dead."

The most important decision and commitment a person will make in his or her life is either to follow Jesus and live to glorify Him or follow Satan and glorify him, because there is no in between. You are either completely giving God authority over your entire life, or you are allowing Satan to manipulate you and destroy your life. The Bible states in Mathew 12:30, "He who is not with me is against me, and he who does not gather with me scatters." God does not want only part of your life, He wants all of it, not because He is a demanding and controlling God, but because he is a jealous God. As Exodus 34:14 states, "Do not worship any other god, for the LORD, whose name is Jealous, is a jealous God." Exodus 20:5 reads, "You shall not bow down to them or worship them; for I, the LORD your God, am a jealous God, punishing the children for the sin of the fathers to the third and fourth generation of those who hate me." Deuteronomy 4:24 states, "For the LORD your God is a consuming fire, a jealous God."; Deuteronomy 6:13-15 states, "Fear the Lord your God, serve him only and take your oath in his name. Do not follow other gods, the gods of the people around you; for the LORD your God, who is among you, is a jealous God and his anger will burn against you, and he will destroy you from the face of the land."

God wants a personal relationship with his children. Just to give an example, there is a twelve-year-old son with his father. The son wakes up, eats, and goes to school without looking to say good morning or goodbye to his father. The father feels unloved and sad. God desires you to call on him first thing in the morning before anything else. Then, the son comes to his dad in the afternoon to ask for help studying for a math exam. The father feels as if he is being used and not truly loved for what he has done and for what he is. Let us reflect this example about ourselves. Do we call on God early in the morning before doing anything else? Is our number one priority giving God glory and praise? Or do we "use" God? Is our relationship with Him based on what we can get or on how we can serve and glorify Him?

We must not allow the enemy to put thoughts in our minds that God understands us for not taking time to speak to Him and ignoring Him either because of lack of time or things we need to do. God gives us every second of our life and helps and protects us. How then can we be so self-centered and call upon the Lord only when we need something? The Bible states in Psalm 47:6, "Sing praises to God, sing praises; sing praises to our King, sing praises." We need to be constantly in prayer with God to draw us closer to Him. The Bible states in 2 Timothy 1:3, "I thank God, whom I serve, as my forefathers did, with a clear conscience, as night and day I constantly remember you in my prayers." We need to pray for God to give us a hunger to know Him and experience Him daily on a deeper level. Mathew 7:21 states, "Not everyone who says to me, 'Lord, Lord,' will enter the kingdom of heaven, but only the one who does the will of my Father who is in heaven."

If anything stops us from reading the Bible or talking to God, we should reject it in the name of Jesus. If we think that the Bible is too hard to understand, we should get one with introductions and commentary. The enemy tells us that it is not important to read the Bible because we attend church on Sundays and if we believe in God, why read about Him? This is a lie of the devil, twisted nonsense. The Bible states in Romans 10:17, "Consequently, faith comes from hearing the message, and the message is heard through the word of Christ." I can assure you that the extra thirty minutes to an hour that we spend with God every morning, in prayer or reading is incredibly more important and life changing than anything else we can do in the whole day. We need to seek what is important and throw away what does not edify our mind and spirit.

We should never let the devil fool us into thinking that because we did something wrong God will not forgive us or love us anymore. God's love for all of us is unconditional. He loved us first, and He created us and gave His only son for us. This was impossible to understand when I suffered depression from removing a medication suddenly during treatment. What happened was that during the end of my treatment I was taking a medication called Lyrica® that helped control my headaches. When I started going to school at M.D. Anderson, I kept forgetting to bring the medication. So, very foolishly and impulsively, I decided to stop taking Lyrica®. I thought that because I was doing fine with cutting a third of the portion (without permission of the doctors or my parents), I would be okay with just removing it entirely. Without asking my mom, who is an I.C.U. nurse, or my dad, who is an Infectious Disease doctor, I abruptly stopped taking Lyrica® without letting anyone know.

About a week and a half later, I changed from having a very positive and happy attitude to being depressed. I showed all the signs of depression. I did nt want to wake up early like I used to. I did not want to eat. I didn't want to talk. I didn't want to read the Bible. I did not want to pray. I did not want to work. I did not want to have any responsibilities. I was never happy, positive or nice. I did not want to shower. I did not want to look pretty. I did not want to go anywhere. All I wanted to do was stay in bed and sleep or watch movies.

This experience was as bad as being treated for a brain tumor. The treatment of cancer was physically hard; depression was emotional and mental hardship. Even though I had everything I needed and wanted in just having a loving family, I felt like I was in the devil's presence all the time when I was depressed. It was the WORST thing that has EVER happened to me.

The enemy worked day and night to try to get me to sin and to blaspheme against God. He constantly insinuated malignant thoughts into my mind. He would suggest things like, "Why don't you stop eating and stop sleeping? No one will miss you when you die. Why are you changing clothes? Stay in your pajamas all day, stay in bed. What are you possibly going to do? It is not worth getting out of bed, Do you actually think that God is going to forgive you for thinking all this? He does not love you, "Why are you going to read the Bible? You are not going to understand it. It's not worth your time. It's too complicated anyway. You already know the Ten Commandments, and everyone hates you already. Why don't you just die?" These are just some of the heinous and corrupting thoughts that the enemy threw into my mind and heart. The second I stopped reading the Bible, the enemy came with more power to try to make me sin. As the word of God states in Luke 11:24-26,[24] "When an impure spirit comes out of a person, it goes through arid places seeking rest and does not find it. Then it says, 'I will return to the house I left.' [25] When it arrives, it finds the house swept clean and put in order. [26] Then it goes and takes seven other spirits more wicked than itself, and they go in and live there. And the final condition of that person is worse than the first." When we are following God but then fall, distract ourselves and stop reading the Bible and praying, the enemy takes advantage of us as our guard is down and returns back with seven more diabolic spirits to make sure that this time he gets a good hold on us.

When my mom noticed my dire depression, she began to make me do chores around the house to occupy my mind with stuff and not let me just sit all day. When she told me to wash clothes, a simple task of separating the whites from the darks, I got anxious over doing it. I remember sitting on the floor of the laundry room thinking to myself: "This is never going to end. Clothes will always need to be washed. I can't do this; this is just one responsibility of life; how could I even do more? How can I live? Better yet, how can I ever become a doctor?"

Having trouble sleeping was an especially serious result of this depression. I was always tired, but I kept thinking, "What if I can't fall asleep?" When it was five o'clock in the morning, I was thinking, "What if I can't sleep tomorrow too?" This pattern continued for an entire week. That week I went without sleep for almost three days in a row. I thought that I was not going to wake up in the morning from a sudden death brought on by fatigue, malnutrition, and dehydration. I ca not adequately explain the dire fatigue I was experiencing throughout that time. But, thank God, He took me out of that depression in time by using my parents, who made me read the Bible and prayed in the morning with me.

During depression, the enemy put thoughts in my mind that he was my friend and God was a mean, demanding father, which was a horrifying lie. My mom kept an eye on me to make sure I was doing something because, as the Bible states in Proverbs 10:4, 4, "Lazy hands make for poverty, but diligent hands bring wealth." My parents eventually found out what caused my depression. That Sunday, when we went to church, the pastor said, "God is the healer and the redeemer; He can heal anything, your illness, depression, etc." All I heard was that He could remove my depression. God spoke to me through my pastor. Even though I was extremely lazy at the time, God helped me, and I began to read the Bible and pray again. I had faith that I was not going to die, and slowly but surely I was back to my old self, but entirely because of God's love and mercy.

The second depression I suffered from was almost as bad as the first one. In the middle of my second depression experience, I was attending Bellaire High School. It was mid-fall semester. I became depressed for almost three months. I stopped giving God the importance He deserved and focused on what I did not have or what I did not or could not do. I felt like I was useless, unwanted, overweight, unloved, and dumb because of my physical condition then. Only later did I realize fully that after the surgeries, I forgot many things that later I remembered when parts of my brain were waking up. I believed false things and lived my life thinking that way. I start thinking that I did not have the capacity to finish all my homework and other studying. I started making simple things much more complicated than they were, like doing laundry. I was silent all the time unless someone spoke to me. My grades began to drop drastically. I stopped caring about my appearance and health because I honestly believed the lie of the devil that I was worthless and going to die soon. As soon as I began having my daily devotional in the morning, as I had before school started and I prayed more, I began to feel useful, loved, beautiful, and smart. Just like God took me out of the first depression by my being obedient and reading the Bible and praying in daily devotionals, He took me out of the second one, thank you Jesus.

The enemy's most powerful force is making you doubt your identity. If we are founded in God's word and what Christ did for us, we have a secure identity as sons and daughters of Christ, and we must not allow anyone or anything to steal it from us. There are several scriptures in the Bible that declare a Christian's identity in Christ such as Jeremiah 29:11, Mathew 16:18, Romans 8:1-2, Philemon 6, Ephesians 1:3-11, Hebrews10: 38-39, 1 Peter 2:5,9-10, 1 Peter 1:23, 2 Timothy 2:21, Romans 8: 28-31, 1 Corinthians 6:11 and 2 Timothy 1:12. They are all clear and understandable, like Jeremiah 29:11: "I have a destiny in God. I know the plans that the Lord has for me are plans to prosper me and not to harm me, plans to give me a hope and a future." As well as Romans 8:1-2, "There is no condemnation in my life because I am in Christ Jesus, because through Christ Jesus the law of the Spirit of life set me free from the law of sin and death. Ephesians 1:3-11 and 3:20 are also beautiful and encouraging. How can the enemy possibly cause us mental harm like depression if we are constantly founded in God's word and promises? We need to stand firm and rebuke the devil in the name of Jesus, because our fight is not with flesh but with principalities of evil, as Ephesians 6:12 talks about; "[12] For our struggle is not against flesh and blood, but against the rulers, against the authorities, against the powers of this dark world and against the spiritual forces of evil in the heavenly realms."

God can use anyone to glorify Him as long as they are willing to serve Him. We need to ask God for forgiveness for our sins, try not to commit them again, and keep going. We should not continue to live in the past. A very wise teacher, Mrs. Barbara Fontenot, once told me, "Paola, you are coming to class too upset all the time. I know the teacher you have before me and how hard she is, but you can't let what happens in there affect the rest of your day. Whatever bad happened throughout your day, leave it where it happened and forget about it." I have never forgotten those wise words said to me by my speech and debate teacher in my freshman year of high school. We cannot let ourselves be upset and bitter the rest of the day over something bad that happened earlier, as Mathew 6:24-26 reads: "Therefore I tell you, do not worry about your life, what you will eat or drink; or about your body, what you will wear. Is not life more important than food, and the body more important than clothes? ^{26}Look at the birds of the air; they do not sow or reap or store away in barns, and yet your heavenly Father feeds them. Are you not much more valuable than they?"

God has changed many sinners and then used them to glorify Him. For example, the disciple Paul, who was a Christian persecutor before he had an encounter with God. In Acts 9:4, the Bible reads, "He fell to the ground and heard a voice say to him, "Saul, Saul, why do you persecute me?" Paul's old name before he got saved was Saul. Once God spoke to him his heart was completely changed and God used him to glorify Him. We also need to ask God for wisdom when we fail and sin. Because we have sinned, no matter what we did, it does not mean that God loves us any less. He loves us the same. He is just waiting for us to repent and keep trying to do what we know is right in God's eyes. When the Apostle Peter betrayed Jesus by denying knowing Him, not once, not twice but three times, he begged God to forgive him. He felt extremely guilty about what he had done, repented for it, and God forgave him. On the other hand, Judas Iscariot also betrayed Jesus by selling Him to the guards for thirty coins of silver, but instead of repenting and asking God's forgiveness, he hanged himself. God forgives you as long as you allow Him to. His grace and mercy are infinite.

Chapter 8

MIRACULOUS

God given miracles are unbelievable, unimaginable, and unexplainable to the human mind. God has shown to be faithful in every situation that I have ever been in, in the good times and the bad, even when I do not realize it. When I was undergoing treatment, my mom would tell me, "Don't worry, when God starts something, He finishes it." Later on, one of the Christian CDs she bought me said, "This time next year, there will be stories to tell." I loved listening to that song because it reminded me that God was soon going to finish this torment and heal me.

What is a miracle? A miracle is something that only God can create, allow, or perform. It is something beyond the comprehension and knowledge of a human. It is knowing that only God could have done it. That is what we knew happened when I woke up alive and healthy after my twelve hour open skull brain surgery. This is one of the grandest miracles God has performed in my life. However, there have been many other miracles that He has allowed me to experience. There were uncountable miracles that I experienced throughout my treatment at M.D. Anderson and that I continue to see in my life thanks only to God and His Son Jesus.

By the end of every chemotherapy treatment, my blood counts would drop because of the toxicity of the medicine. In order to keep the patient safe, treatment requires either the Neupogen or Neulasta shot after treatment. These shots cause the bone marrow to begin to reproduce white and red blood cells. The normal white blood cell count is 5.1-15.5 K/UL; the normal red blood cell count is 3.40-4.70 M/UL; the normal hemoglobin counts are 9.5- 13.3 G/DL and the normal platelet count is 159-353K/UL.

If my hemoglobin went anywhere below an 8, I would get severe headaches, the lower it went, the worse the pain of the headache. These headaches limited me in many ways. Any sort of movements made my head hurt more. It limited me as the hydrocephalus headaches did, except to a different extent of pain. Walking fast made my head hurt more, I was limited to walk and move at a glacial speed in order not to prevent pain in my head. The pain also augmented when I got up and out of my bed, bended over, sat down, moved my head to look in any direction, looking down, as well as any noise.

If my white blood cells went low, then my immune system became weaker, which meant I was more likely to be infected. Everywhere I went and stayed had to be completely immaculate. If my blood counts went low, I had to wear a mask and gloves to prevent from getting any type of infections. Everything I ate or drank had to be made with gloves on or washed and sanitized hands. It would be life threatening to get infected while your white blood cells where low.

When I was in one of my chemotherapy treatments, my white blood counts dropped dramatically. The doctors ordered the Neulasta shot, but it didn't work, my counts stayed low. Even though everything around me in the hospital was clean and everything I ate came from the room service at M.D. Anderson, I got a fever. My mom told me that even if I wanted to, not to go under the covers, but to put the air in the room as cold as I could handle it (55 degrees Fahrenheit) and not to put sheets over myself because I could have a septic shock. We prayed for God to increase my counts.

Our family prayed in faith constantly, for my white blood counts to go up. The next morning at 4 a.m., my nurse came to my room to draw labs. Later that morning, she came with my CBC, or complete blood count. As I scrolled down the page, I noticed that the White Cell count was not highlighted in alert red anymore. Without the use of another painful Neulasta shot, God raised my counts! I was so unexplainably amazed and thankful! The doctors said it must have been a technical problem with the computer, but I knew it was God.

One of the last times I got the Neulasta shot, God proved Himself again as being a faithful, loving, and caring Father. I remember like it was today, my mom and brothers were in the room when the nurse came in to give me the shot. Usually the shot would make me yell loud enough for other nurses on the floor to come see what was happening to me. When it was injected slowly it literally felt like a poisonous snake biting me with its sharp fangs, but when it was injected fast it truly felt like an atomic bomb going off while crushing blades of metal drenched in with burning acid.

So that day, we tried doing something different, we prayed for God to take away all the pain from the shot with faith that He was going to do it. It was hard seeing that needle with that thick medicine in the syringe and say, "God I trust you and you alone; I know that you are going to take away all the pain from the shot, I have the complete trust and faith in You that You can and You will not allow me to feel any pain in the name of your Son, Jesus! Thank you Father."

I remember I was continuing to pray when I felt the nurse put the Band-Aid on. I stopped and luridly said, "That was it, you did it?" The nurse simply said, "Yep, all done." I called all my relatives and told them of another miracle God had done for me. I was more excited about God's miracle than the pain I did not feel. No one can ever tell me that there is no power in prayer or that God does not exist, because I have experienced His miracles and have felt His presence. The enemy can try to make us doubt what God says, whom He is and what He can do, but we should grab on to God like our life depended on it, which it actually does. God is so full of love, mercy, and grace. He even spoiled me in something as small as taking the pain away from a shot. I can almost assure you that God would not have done what He did if we did not believe that He would do it. His word says that we need to have faith in Him, always, no matter the situation. Hebrews 11:1 reads, "[1]Now faith is being sure of what we hope for and certain of what we do not see."

Another false claim is that miracles do not happen since Jesus left. I have experienced, seen, and heard of miracles around the world. Jesus said that if we had faith we could make miracles like the ones He did and greater ones. John 14:12 declares, "[12] Very truly I tell you, whoever believes in me will do the works I have been doing, and they will do even greater things than these, because I am going to the Father." The Bible states in Mathew 17:20, He replied, "Because you have so little faith. I tell you the truth, if you have faith as small as a mustard seed, you can say to this mountain, 'Move from here to there' and it will move. Nothing will be impossible for you." I have had the blessing to have met several pastors and church members that have healed people from diabolic spirits, physical illness, and emotional sickness, thank God.

Several pastors and other Christians have healed chronic diseases and infections, in the name of Jesus, around the world. There are so many examples I can talk about! For example, a kid at my church laid hands on a friend's shoulders, which had had an accident playing football. He was only about twelve years old and two other bough teens rammed into both his shoulders. His shoulder blades crunched and bone shattered into pieces. The doctors said that he wouldn't be able to move his shoulders anymore in his life. So, when my friend was worshiping at church, God spoke to his heart and told him to go massage his injured friend's shoulder's. He was skeptical at first, but then God told him again to go do it, through the Holy Spirit, so he did. While he was doing it, they heard a loud snap. Worried that he had hurt him, his friend lifted his hands and began to wave them in ecstasy screaming out, "I can move my arms, I can move them!"

Another example of a divine healing touch was my other Christian friend's mother who had her heart literally torn in half in an accident. When the surgeons when in to try to fix it she had a stroke, so they went to her head. This happened twice in each part of the brain, but her family kept praying for her. Then, the doctors came to her family and told them not to expect her to stay alive for the next day. That night, her family fasted and prayed in faith for her to leave the hospital completely healed, knowing that God is above EVERY circumstance. The next day, the doctors unexpectedly let her go home, because she was unexplainably healed. If someone still believes that God does not perform miracles there are several fascinating miraculous stories on Google when you search healing miracles about God's healing touch and love.

We tend to focus on the huge miracles, and tend to forget the "smaller" ones. Just the fact that we are healthy and can read this book is a miracle. Being able to live and do everything in our life is allowed by God. We need to focus on the "smaller" miracles that God does for us such as: being able to walk, talk, sleep, eat, think straight; they are all blessings, but we need to see that we live in a miracle in which God has made us in every way that we are. Being alive and having the opportunity to know Christ is alone enough for us to worship God every moment of the day. We do not deserve his love, mercy, grace and we definitely do not deserve to exists and be redeemed by His only Son's inhumane and cruel death. Just take a second to think, God, all-powerful, all glorious, all loving and caring chose to create us in His image, even though He doesn't need us in any way. He is such a loving God that He gave up his <u>ONLY</u> son for us. In order for us to have the chance to be saved and go into His kingdom, He did it for us, human sinners, who most of us in this world don't even believe in!! How can we possibly allow the enemy to blindfold us to this extent where the Christian religion is one of the lowest populated today?

It is not normal to be healthy, to drive, to have a house, cars, a bed, food, cloths, a working healthy brain, etc. Our culture uses the media to try to make us think that the only way to gain happiness is to be wealthy and have many new material things. Satan uses the media and anything else he has to make you feel like a failure in every way. The American dream has misguided many people in thinking that happiness and contentment can be bought. There will always be something missing inside of you until you give all your life to Jesus, because He made us with a purpose to have a personal relationship with Him and not to focus and grow in relationship with any sort of material objects.

Chapter 9

CHALLENGE OVER CHALLENGE

After the sixth chemotherapy treatment, my body was exhausted from all the different types of drugs I was receiving. I had pain in my kidneys, from the Cyclophosphamide, I had real minor permanent damage in my right ear from the Cisplatin and I could not tolerate any more nausea. It was my body's way of saying, enough is enough. Seven months after my last chemotherapy, my audiology technician told me that she did not know what happened, but the permanent damage in my ear was gone and that both my ears were perfectly healthy, thank God.

After three weeks of my sixth cycle of chemotherapy, I was praying for our doctor to tell us that my body had gone through enough treatment. I was praying not to finish all eight cycles because of all the pain and nausea I was going through.

The Power of Standing in Faith

Four days before my seventh inpatient chemotherapy, Hurricane Ike was coming towards Galveston, Texas. It was a Thursday morning and my mom and I were waiting in the clinic's waiting room for an appointment. While we were there, the news came on TV in front of us, showing the weather in Galveston, two days before the expectance of the arrival of Hurricane Ike in the city. The moment my mom saw those waves, she told me that we had to evacuate that night. So, we went to talk to my doctors to see what we were going to do about the chemotherapy. The doctors were understanding and told us that the clinic would be closed; however, that the hospital was safe enough to stay at and that several patients were staying to receive treatment.

After rescheduling everything, we went home to pack. My dad searched the web for available destinations and found that Santa Fe, New Mexico had a vacancy for a week. Since it was less than a year from having my brain surgery, flying there was out of the question, because the pressure in the plane would give me severe pains in my sensitive head. It was a fun, long, and an interesting drive. I felt like God was using the hurricane to allow us to have some sort of vacation and for me to recover more from the sixth cycle of chemotherapy.

When we got back from our relaxing evacuation vacation, we went to the clinic for an appointment with my doctor. We told him the truth, my body could not continue with two more chemotherapy inpatient treatments. We told him about my pains and symptoms. Thank God I had an understanding and wise doctor. He decided that I could not stop at the sixth cycle, but since I was in so much pain and so weak, he said that we could finish the last two cycles with chemotherapeutic pills. After hearing the doses of the medication and the symptoms, I rapidly agreed to finish my treatment with chemotherapeutic pills. To avoid nausea, I took the chemo pills after dinner, so I would have the nausea when I was already asleep. Completely thanking God, I did not have increased nausea for my last two chemotherapy treatments.

Every day since my hair fell out, I prayed to Jesus for Him to allow it to grow faster than ever before and for it to change from being wavy to curly and from it being auburn to black. I loved my hair before, but it bothered me when several people commented on the different colors on my head. I had dark black eyebrows, natural red highlights growing at the sides of my hairline and my hair was brown. So growing up, I had many questions about dying my hair, which bothered me, which it should not have. So, out of curiosity, I looked up in the internet how long it took for hair to start growing after it falling all off, because of chemotherapy. The statistics said that it usually took 4-5 months after your last chemotherapy treatment for your hair to start growing back. The doctors said the same thing. I kept praying for a miracle that my hair would grow sooner. Before I finished my 7th cycle of chemotherapy, my hair was already growing back! It grew black and curly, as I had prayed for. After a few months I realized how unique my natural red highlights were with my brown hair and black eyebrows and wanted them back. After praying about it for weeks, I went to get my trims cut. After the haircut, my curls went away and my hair started to look more and more auburn throughout the month and now I finally see my natural red highlights growing again! Even in the most tiny and meaningless things, God is faithful and loves us enough to care about our desires in EVERY circumstance.

I could not have been happier when I finished the final eighth cycle of chemotherapy!!! It was in the end of November of 2008. I called all our relatives and family friends to let them know that thank God I finally finished the chemotherapy treatment. If I could have jumped up and down with my head not hurting I would have done it until I went to sleep. It was irrevocably ethereal.

After the last chemotherapy treatment I had to attend several checkups to make sure there was no sign of malignant cancer cells in my body. I attended an audiology appointment, an ophtalmology appointment, a couple different M.R.I appointments, I had blood drawn, a lumbar puncture, and a follow up with my main doctors, Dr. Wolff and Dr. Fullbright. We had the faith that God completely healed me, but protocol needs proof.

It was a complete miracle. All the test came out immaculately normal. My neurosurgeon even said that from viewing the M.R.I visual results, he could not even tell that there was a tumor in my head, thank God. Only God can heal you completely from any sickness or disease especially when you have faith in Him and it is His will to do so.

So now that I am completely done with treatment, I have periodic checkups, to make sure that I do not relapse, or get the cancer again. I am a hundred percent positive that I will never have this cancer again, because of the faith that God has given me in Him. As I said earlier, it is protocol to scientifically document that I am continually in remission, or staying completely healthy.

My checkup started every two weeks, then, they moved to being every month, to every three months, then every six months, then, every year, then, after five years of the last treatment and I am pretty sure that the final checkup is after five years. I just finished my post three-month checkups and the next ones will be in six months, if God permits.

Chapter 10

A NEW BEGINNING

It is incredible what God can do. It is breathtaking to experience His love and power. We are the ones who choose not to take His blessings and power when we doubt Him. Why do we stress, why do we choose to carry all the burdens when Jesus has already taken them for us? Philippians 4:6-7 reads, "Do not be anxious about anything, but in everything, by prayer and petition, with thanksgiving, present your request upon the Lord." And as Mathew 11:28-30 states, "Come to me, all you who are weary and burdened, and I will give you rest. ^{29}Take my yoke upon you and learn from me, for I am gentle and humble in heart, and you will find rest for your souls. ^{30}For my yoke is easy and my burden is light."

Before we stress or worry, we need to ask God to help us put our absolute trust in Him, because He is going to take care of it, according to His perfect will, for our greater good. Once we ask for it, we need to work for it. We are not going to sit at home and pray for a million dollars with out doing anything. As James 2:26 reads, "For as the body without the spirit is dead, so faith without works is dead also." We need to do our best in everything we do according to God's word. Ecclesiastes 9:10 reads, "Whatever your hand finds to do, do it with all your might, for in the grave, where you are going, there is neither working nor planning nor knowledge nor wisdom." Once I do my best, I have absolute peace, because I have the complete faith that God is going to take care of everything for me. As 1 John 5:14 reads, "This is the confidence we have in approaching God: that if we ask anything according to his will, he hears us."

Everything in my life has completely shifted in an absolute 360 degrees turn, once I gave my entire life to Jesus. I used to be an obsessive type "A" person. Everything I did had to be the best and there was never any room for mistakes. I was stressfully competitive in everything I did. For example, I used to run three miles in the morning, three miles in the evening, I would swim laps three to five times a week for thirty minutes. I went to kickboxing classes, salsa classes, and occasionally I would go bike riding. I would also study as much as possible, stress about getting only A's, and even cheated once because I wanted to get a hundred and seven on a test and not a ninety-seven! Now that God has changed me, I do not kill myself trying to reach an impossible goal. I exercise daily, but I give myself brakes when I need them. My goal is to be fit, not to be Wonder Woman.

I used to stress every day over meaningless and unnecessary situations. For example, if I had any type of quiz or test, I would worry if it was going to be hard and then, I would fret while I was taking it and then I would be anxious while waiting to see the results. I used to worry about events far in the future. Stress handcuffed my life. Now I am living one day at a time in peace as scripture reads in Mathew 6:34, "Therefore do not worry about tomorrow, for tomorrow will worry about itself. Each day has enough trouble of its own." Now that I am living for God, I try my best to leave all my needs and worries at his feet every day. The breaking of that bondage has truly allowed me to experience true freedom at heart, all my faith and trust is in God alone.

I used to be intolerably arrogant and selfish. I yelled, disobeyed, and was rude to my parents. I thought that since I had good grades, attended a challenging magnet school, had many friends, and was very athletic, I was superior to others. I actually believed that I was better than other people at my school, because I made better grades and had more "important" friends. I was living in a complete lie of the devil.

Before God changed me, I thought a few people were extremely annoying, selfish, weird, and hated a couple of them. The things that they said and did made me so frustrated on the inside, which just caused me to dislike them even more. I used to despise some family friends for what they did and for what they said. The "old me" truly died once I start living completely for God. God gave me love for all those people that had hurt me emotionally one way or the other and for all those people that I found annoying. God gave me so much love for the people I could not tolerate that I even contacted a few of them and told them that I was sorry if I had ever offended them in anyway. They kindly replied the same thing that I asked them. God gave me so much love and forgiveness for them that I even called this one girl that I used to truly dislike, to come have lunch with my other friends and I, so she could hear about the power and love of God and the testimony God had given me. God gave me a passion to spread His word and to save other people's eternities. Now, anywhere I go, I look for chances to give my testimony and speak about God's love, power, and mercy in a wise way. There is not a cell in my body or any part of my spirit ashamed of speaking about God anymore, thank God. On the contrary, my whole heart and soul desires to live for Him and Him alone, no matter what anyone says or thinks. I have truly laid down my life and followed Him as Mathew 16:24 reads, "Then Jesus said to his disciples, "If anyone would come after me, he must deny himself and take up his cross and follow me", only by God's mercy and redeeming love.

Before I was saved, I was completely terrified and embarrassed of speaking of God. I remember one time I went out to eat with two close friends. We went to a popular Mexican restaurant on a Friday night. The moment our plates came, one of my friends, Hillary, extended her arms towards us to pray for our food. I was so luridly and unexplainably embarrassed. As my heart was pounding of humiliation, I extended my arms and closed my eyes. God changed me entirely once I was saved. After I was diagnosed, I went back to New Orleans and God allowed me to share my testimony several times to many different people. The first time I went, I invited only about five to seven friends to come eat at a restaurant near the Tulane campus. When I went I extended my arms to pray for our food and everyone joined hands. The second time I went, there were four tables pulled together and much harder for everyone to pray at the same time, but I did it anyway and God spoke through me and I shared my testimony. Only God could have changed me in wanting to give my testimony and speak about God's miracles and love. Even though there were people throughout the table that looked at me as if I were insane and some even left the table laughing in the middle of my testimony. Instead of feeling embarrassed or let down when that person did that, I had an even greater desire and motivation to speak about God. All spirit of shyness is gone. All I have is an evident desire to glorify God in everything I do, no matter what it takes!

God created the skies, the ocean, animals, nature, and our entire existence, as the book of Genesis reads. Why should we allow other things, events, or people be higher in our priority list than God who has given us everything? Everything that is valued down here is not valued up there. This life is just a microscopic test to earn eternal life. We should not love God and do what He says because we do not want to go to hell. We should love and pursue God for whom He is and for what He has done for us. We are NOTHING compared to Him and deserve NOTHING from Him. Even though we do not deserve His love, mercy, or grace, He has sent his ONLY son for us to have an opportunity to know Him and experience salvation. We do not only have to say that we are Christian. We have to put his word into practice in our daily lives. People are secretly praising God underground in China and other foreign countries, in order for them not to be persecuted, but how can we not make the time out of our day, which God gives us, to worship Him? You make time for what you think is important, the choice is yours.

www.ingramcontent.com/pod-product-compliance
Ingram Content Group UK Ltd.
Pitfield, Milton Keynes, MK11 3LW, UK
UKHW041954230426
12048UKWH00008B/326